A
CRISIS
OF

OBSTACLES TO
CHALLENGES TO
REASONS TO

HOPE

IN
THE
MODERN
WORLD

Ed Wojcicki

Foreword by Henri J. M. Nouwen

THE THOMAS MORE PRESS
Chicago, Illinois

ISBN 0-88347-253-8

ACKNOWLEDGMENTS

The author and publisher are grateful to the following for permission to include copyrighted material:

DONAHUE: MY OWN STORY by Donahue and Company. Copyright © 1979 by Phil Donahue. Reprinted by permission of Simon & Schuster, Inc.

From WORKING: *People Talk About What They Do All Day and How They Feel About What They Do,* by Studs Terkel. Copyright © 1972, 1974 by Studs Terkel. Reprinted by permission of Pantheon Books, a division of Random House, Inc.

From PATHFINDERS by Gail Sheehy. Copyright © 1981 by Gail Sheehy. Reprinted by permission of William Morrow & Co.

From WITH OPEN HANDS by Henri Nouwen. Copyright © 1972 by Henri Nouwen. Reprinted by permission of Ave Maria Press, Notre Dame, Ind.

From HEALING WOUNDED EMOTIONS by Martin H. Padovani. Copyright © 1987 by Martin H. Padovani. Reprinted by permission of Twenty-Third Publications, Mystic CT 06355-0180.

From REACHING OUT by Henri Nouwen. Copyright © 1975 by Henri Nouwen. Reprinted by permission of Double-

TABLE OF CONTENTS

DEDICATION

To anyone with a spark of hope;
and to cynics,
who know deep down
they have another choice.

ACKNOWLEDGMENTS

PUTTING a book together and finding the words to say exactly what I mean would be an impossible project for me to handle by myself.

First of all, I am indebted to my wife and best friend, Sally, who knows better than I how many chores went undone and how many little things were taken care of just so that I could continue writing. It's worth noting that this manuscript was put together in a very hectic year when Sally and her partner were opening their own advertising and promotional display business.

I am very grateful to those who read drafts of the initial chapters and then offered their criticism to help refine my understanding and definition of hope as it applies to everyday living. Most instrumental in this area was my brother Ted (older and therefore wiser than I), who managed to break away from his own busy schedule. One time he even agreed to drive to meet me at a place midway between our two cities so that we could discuss the manuscript.

Also, I am greatly appreciative to Father Richard Chiola and Beth Murphy, O.P., who supported me immensely and also offered many crucial insights to steer and direct my arguments.

And to several others I am grateful, too. They would probably be surprised to know how very much their support, encouragement and occasional suggestions of sources meant to me along the way. I'm thinking of friends like Dick Whitworth, Carla Fisher, Linda Cook, Rick Wade, and Lou Jacquet (Lou, by the way, had the gumption to tell me to come up with a better title than the one I started with. It was great advice.)

Many others supported me, too, such as other family members and the small but wonderful staff of people with whom I work day after day (when I am actually in the office and not at another meeting) at *Catholic Times* in Springfield.

These people taught me that I cannot write a book in isolation. Some of their own ideas have made it onto these pages, a fact which I hope is another way of letting them know how much I value their insights.

FOREWORD

ED WOJCICKI and I have never met! Still we are soul-friends. Our friendship began four years ago when Ed, in his capacity as editor, wrote an open letter to me in the *Catholic Times* of the Diocese of Springfield, Illinois. The warm, personal, conversational tone of that letter and the letters that followed, open letters as well as letters that were personal and private, made it very easy to come to know him, to listen to what he had to say and to think about him as a friend.

I was, therefore, quite honored to be invited to write a foreword to his first book. And reading Ed's reflections on obstacles, challenges and reasons to hope, I felt as though I were reading one of Ed's personal letters to me. As he wrote about fear and anger, frustration and bitterness, he was speaking to me in a very intimate and gentle way, reminding me of things I knew about and even wrote about, but kept forgetting about in my everyday life. His words about hope as "a virtue badly needed as we peer into the 21st Century and the next millenium," stirred up within me something very important.

This book is a truly pastoral work. It touches our wounds carefully and never condemns; it shows our pain lovingly, always with a twinkle in the eye; it helps us to look compassionately at our own weaknesses as well as the weaknesses of others, and, most of all, it states clearly and unambiguously that we have a choice to make, a choice to hope.

Choose hope! That is what this book says, not only in general, but also in very concrete and practical terms. As I reflect on the effect of Ed Wojcicki's book on me, I am amazed at how much I need to be called to make the inner choice for hope over and over again. Faced with countless daily temptations to despair of myself, my family, friends, colleagues, my Church and society, choosing hope requires of me a true spiritual discipline.

By way of introducing *A Crisis of Hope,* I want to say a few words about the spiritual discipline of choosing hope. It might seem a strange idea that we can choose hope. When we think of our experience with such deep emotions as fear, bitterness, anger and despair on the one hand, and joy, peace, forgiveness and hope on the other, it seems that we have little control over them. They emerge from the deepest places of our heart and often present themselves to us long before we can make any decision about them. We find ourselves being angry or forgiving, despairing or hopeful, without having made any decision in the matter.

We say often: ''He makes me angry'' or ''She gives me hope'' or ''That plunged me into despair'' or ''This truly made me joyful again.'' We often suggest to ourselves and others that we have little choice in the matter of our responses to what happens around us. But this book shows convincingly that we **do** have a choice. We can choose forgiveness, joy, peace and hope, instead of revenge, sadness, anger and despair. What makes us human is precisely that we have minds and hearts able to choose not only objects, partners,

12

careers and life-styles, but also our interior responses to the world in which we live. We can choose to be hopeful. Hopefulness is not located somewhere outside of ourselves. It is an inner response which we can regulate. Here we touch the center of the biblical faith: Our lives are not based on fate, but on choice. We are not victims, but masters of our own destiny. In *Deuteronomy* (30:19), God says: "Today, I call heaven and earth to witness against you: I am offering you life or death, blessing or curse. Choose life, then, so that you and your descendants may live."

Our great temptation remains to live as though we don't have a choice and to behave like pitiful victims of circumstances over which we have no control. The great spiritual challenge is to claim our inner freedom to choose life, joy, peace and hope.

This requires real discipline. Before we know it, we find ourselves complaining about all the bad things that happen to us, gossiping about people who hurt our feelings or damage our career, commiserating about the bad times in which we live or the evil powers that surround us. Before we know it, we have given up the freedom of choice to live our lives from within and to respond to our world according to our knowledge of who we are and who we want to become.

I have a friend who travels a lot, meets people in the most diverse circumstances and has seen immense poverty and destruction. Every time he returns from a trip, I expect him to tell me how awful, how depressing, discouraging and hopeless were the situations that he witnessed. I expect him to respond as most newspapers do: with long descriptions of the increasing problems that face our world. He never does.

13

Instead, he always has a story of hope to share. He talks about meeting small groups of people who live peacefully among suffering men and women. He talks about little initiatives of compassion. He talks about a child who was saved from death, a woman who shared the little she had with her visitors, a young man who spoke about God's love, a monk who radiated peace and joy, a handicapped man who, after years of care, could walk again and even say a few words . . . small, seemingly insignificant events that I myself might never have noticed, but which for him are true signs of hope.

The more I listen to this friend, the more I realize that he has chosen hope. He never ignores or denies the hard realities of life, but he does not allow them to lead him into despair. He keeps discovering and lifting up the countless small treasures of love hidden in the dark soil and is always grateful for their beauty. The mystery of it all is that in his presence you gradually learn to see new sources of hope and, once you have learned to recognize them, you come to see more and more of them.

Every choice for hope makes the next choice easier. Just as joy brings forth joy, and love brings forth love, so hope always brings forth hope. But nothing happens automatically; it always requires a conscious choice. Two people may be involved in the same accident. For one it becomes the end of happiness; for the other the beginning of joy. We can seldom change the circumstances, but we can always choose the way we respond to them and give them a place in our ongoing journey. Failure, disappointment, loss, illness, violence and war, they all can make us angry and resentful and send us to our graves as disillusioned people who didn't

14

get what we deserved. But it does not have to be that way. We have the choice to let those painful events purify our hearts and minds and set us free to discover the deeper resources of life often hidden below the ups and downs of our daily existence.

But is there any reality behind all this, or are we dealing here simply with mind games? Are we simply choosing to look at the sunny side of life, even when "reality" says that there is a lot more reason for despair than for hope? Is choosing hope nothing but positive thinking in a negative living world? In the final analysis, is the choice for hope little more than a form of psychological athletics that trains us into a self-serving, selective perception of our reality? Are the St. Francis's, the Mother Teresas, the Martin Luther Kings and Dorothy Days of our time nothing but men and women who, in spite of the horrendous darkness that confronts them, cling naively to their illusions of a better world? In short: Is hope built on anything real? If not, then it is little more than mental gymnastics on the part of people who simply don't want to face reality.

But true hope is built, not on illusions, but on a *promise*. And it is the promise that makes living with hope radically different from wishful thinking. We can choose to hope in the midst of a despairing world because there is a promise that reaches out far beyond the ebb and flow of the good and the bad moments of our lives. Without a promise, there can be no hope. This promise was given to Adam and Eve, to Abraham and Sarah, to Noah, to Jacob and Rebecca, to Moses and the prophets. It is the promise that filled the heart of Jesus who said: "Look, I am with you always, yes, to

15

the end of time'' (*Matthew* 28:20). It is this promise that has nurtured and sustained all the great men and women who overcame their despair and chose for hope against all seeming odds.

This promise assures us that, when all battles are fought, all losses counted, all gains collected, all pains suffered and all joys fully tasted—yes, when all has been said and everything done—life will prove itself stronger than death, love stronger than fear, God stronger than all demons.

I am deeply convinced that it is this promise that forms the hidden foundation of Ed Wojcicki's life and the invisible force that allowed him to write this marvelous book.

As Ed's letters to me were the beginning of a new friendship and a new *hope,* so I hope and pray that all those who read this book will read it as a caring letter from a friend who desires nothing more and nothing less than to offer hope.

Henri J.M. Nouwen

INTRODUCTION

I frequently run into cynical people. And sarcastic people. And frustrated people. In fact, this book started out more than a year ago as an essay on cynicism, one of my favorite topics. But I soon discovered I would rather write about hope.

The timing seemed right.

Euphoria about blossoming freedom in the world was heading toward a climax in 1990. It was a time of optimism unseen since the end of World War II, many were saying. But now that things have changed so drastically again, I find myself reflecting on three questions about hope. I come up with three different answers:

Is this really a time of great hope in the world? Maybe not.

Are people more hopeful than ever as they go about their daily affairs? No.

Should they be? Yes.

Maybe not, no and yes. Having three different answers complicates my task of reflecting on hope against a backdrop of modern cynicism.

Most of my focus in this book will be on ordinary people and rather timeless ordinary situations to which they can relate.

But I cannot dive into the topic without a brief digression into the context of modern history we are now creating. After the Berlin Wall came down late in 1989—the most dramatic early sign of the disintegration of the Cold War—East and West Germany reunified a year later. Then, just before Thanksgiving 1990, the Cold War supposedly ended with a treaty signed triumphantly by 34 nations.

Also contributing to the worldwide optimism last year was the February 1990 release of longtime political prisoner Nelson Mandela in South Africa. Freedom, it seemed, was catching on.

But by January 1991, events were damping world euphoria. Economic problems mounted in the Soviet Union; shelves there were bare; people were gloomy. Then Soviet troops rolled in and forcibly attempted to put the brakes on Lithuanians', Latvians' and Estonians' ambitions for complete independence.

Also tempering the euphoria was the sudden, massive deployment of U.S. troops to Saudi Arabia in the summer of 1990, following Iraq's invasion of Kuwait. Would there be war? Yes, the U.N.-sanctioned war against Iraq began in mid-January 1991, with the American people's widespread support tempered by fears of massive bloodshed. The war lasted just six weeks; Kuwait was liberated. But as I write this immediately after the war, it is far too early to know its long-term consequences on the Middle East.

With the war still fresh on our minds and Soviet troops maintaining an aggressive presence in the Baltics, it clearly is not the best, most peaceful, most hopeful of times in the world. But with Saddam Hussein evidently in check in Iraq and with new proposals now emerging for the dismantling of apartheid in South Africa, it clearly is not the worst of times, either.

A CRISIS OF HOPE

On to my second question: Are people more hopeful than ever?

No, definitely not.

Look closer to home. For most Americans, their general attitude about life is determined not so much by great international events as by what happens in their daily activities.

They are concerned about the stability and health of their families. They grow anxious when someone gets cancer or the prospect of divorce suddenly looms.

They always have a nagging concern about the security of their jobs and level of their income. They get anxious when their careers begin to stagnate or when the newspapers keep talking about an oncoming recession.

They are concerned about the quality of life in their local community, about their family's role and place in the local social order (are they and their children accepted?), and about the effectiveness of organizations in which they are volunteers (is their effort really making a difference?).

The more uncertain or negative these are, the more people tend to say their general feeling is one of frustration or unhappiness or anger. I am regularly around people whose sour attitude toward life is dominated by one of these negative feelings. Frustration is epidemic, and it is contagious.

(For a few people, of course, their most recent golf score is just as important to their mood as any of these things.)

I found it interesting that the same day page one of my daily newspaper was announcing the reunification of Germany (Oct. 3, 1990), columnist Ellen Goodman was describing in the opinion pages a very worried and unsettled American middle class. She had just traveled around the country and talked with many people. "There is a bad case of jitters going around," she wrote. "For the first time in my memory people believe that many systems are breaking down at the same time. . . . It is clear that the feeling good era is over. No one is whistling 'Don't Worry, Be Happy' any more. In America, even the well are worried."[1]

Goodman's description is accurate. Many people are worried, concerned, frustrated. About their jobs, about their relationships, about the failures of leadership in their government, communities and churches. They are tempted to give in to frustration, to bitterness, to hopelessness.

Should more people be more hopeful?

I say it bluntly: Yes, of course! Not necessarily optimistic, but hopeful. The two are not the same.

Not enough people, perhaps very few, have enough hope. And too many people, drooling with cynicism, gain too much influence with their nay-saying cries of despair.

I have hope. I am a person of hope.

I have been without hope. I have been frustrated by people's meanness and insensitivity. I still get frustrated.

I have been self-righteous, disillusioned, bitter, sinfully cynical and sarcastic. I still am, sometimes.

But mostly, and usually, and generally, I feel at my core a great need to hope. Some days hope is all I have as I observe evil, irresponsibility and deception in the world.

I take my cue from the Old Testament story of a widow at Zarephath. A very poor woman, she answered the door one day and found Elijah asking for some bread. She said she had nothing to offer. "I have nothing baked," she told Elijah. "There is only a handful of flour in my jar and a little oil in my jug. Just now I was collecting a couple of sticks, to go in and prepare something for myself and my son; when we have eaten it, we shall die'' (1 *Kings* 17:12).

The woman did not realize what a little generosity would do for her. After the woman baked a small cake for Elijah, God blessed her by making sure the jar of flour and jug of oil miraculously restocked itself to keep the woman well-nourished for a year.

The woman was at the breaking point; she assumed the few resources she had were practically useless, and so she could predict bluntly, ''We shall die.'' How much her lack of hope, rooted in the reality of her poverty, is comparable to the voices of doomsayers all around us today. Modern-day complainers love to generalize that a great institutional downfall is at hand; they find dozens of reasons to say their country, their church or their community is on the skids. And many believe they know precisely where most of the blame lies. If only television would have less trash. . . . If only American companies were as industrious as the Japanese. . . . If only the media were not so biased against religion. . . . If only the nuns still wore their habits. . . . If only preachers would practice what they preach. . . . If only the unions would be less pushy. . . . If only corporate managers would pursue an increase in productivity rather than leveraged buyouts. . . . If only society placed less emphasis on material things. . . . If only young parents spent more time with their children. . . .

If more people would only see just how much they themselves are projecting the blame for society's ills on an outside, often institutional, power, and would reflect instead on the contribution they could make, buoyed by an indestructible foundation of hope, they might begin to understand how much lasting power and hope there is in a handful of flour.

The first thing they should understand is that there is no such thing as a life without stress, or a life without its ups and downs. Life's circumstances contribute to our stress and even lead to a certain amount of distress. We normally and naturally feel angry, fearful, confused and frustrated at times. We feel stress, and every time we do, we have a choice about whether we are going to deal with those feelings and work through them. We choose how we will respond.

We can respond with a sense of hope, or we can ultimately live in bitterness, continually blaming the world around us for every painful feeling we have. This is a book about hope, but it is not a book about how to get rid of stress, because that is impossible and not even desirable. As I will explain, people with high levels of satisfaction about their lives often go through very difficult times and later conclude that the major problems presented a challenge, not a fatal blow. Neither is this a book about how to be happy, nor about a shortcut to self-gratification. I have long maintained that a goal of "being happy" is unreasonable, because happiness is a byproduct of how we live, not something in and of itself that we can work for. A craving for immediate gratification or immediate rewards for what we do, in fact, can be an enemy of hope.

While an attitude of hope is one that we can choose, it is important to note up front that hopelessness has many disguises. Hope has many potential enemies, many obstacles. The feelings that all of us experience naturally in response to challenges and crises in the world around us provide temptations to lead us away from hope. If we can learn to identify and articulate these feelings for what they are—anger, anxiety, frustration, bitterness, confusion and so on—we will learn not only that these are sometimes appropriate, but also that we can use them as tools for personal growth.

Left unattended, however, the feelings can lead us on a downward spiral and into hopelessness, despair, or worst of all, cynicism.

Signs of hopelessness and people without much hope can be found in all of the significant social settings in which we operate on a daily basis: in families, in our local communities, in the government, on the job and in our churches. I have observed a great deal of this on the front row of life that I have had as a reporter and editor for more than a dozen years. What is most interesting is that the same kinds of organizational and interpersonal problems that many people believe are unique to their kind of work and personal experiences are actually quite common across the board. In just about any setting, people question the quality of leadership. In every setting, people grumble that somebody else is not carrying his or her load. People in offices moan that the boss does not care about the employees, and people in the pews complain that the pastor is not sensitive enough. People seem angry that ''businesses care only about profits'' and that pastors ''ask for money all the time.'' And people are muttering all too often that there is no reason to hope for anything better.

Everywhere are the cries of hopelessness; needed very badly are bold whispers of hope.

Ed Wojcicki

My perspective is that of a journalist, but it goes beyond that. My range of personal life experiences has taken me into periods of bewildering despair as well as significant moments of hope. Much of my case for hope is built on my professional and personal experiences, with the support of psychological and human development experts. Many of my examples are from family, job and political experiences, my own and those of others. But my frame of reference goes beyond these categories and into the realm of the spiritual, and more particularly, my upbringing as a Roman Catholic. While I do not argue that hope is exclusively a Christian virtue, I do conclude that God is the source of my hope and that his relationship with the human race is the consummate reason for having hope.

The presence or absence of hope in church institutions is an especially salient issue at this time. The scandals of many television evangelists has cast a pall over all of organized religion in America, even though some of these preachers are not directly linked to any denomination. The publicity surrounding the scandals of ministers arrested for pedophilia have also contributed to suspicions about organized religion.

Beyond the highly publicized scandals, there is a more important reason, even closer to home, that a wavering hope in the institutional church needs to be examined. This has to do with what happens to people who take several steps forward by getting quite active in church activities or becoming church employees. In the Roman Catholic Church, there has been an explosion in the growth of official lay involvement since the mid-1960s, propelled by Vatican II reforms and a declining number of priests. This has resulted in more

24

lay people assuming positions of leadership at the parish and diocesan levels. In theory, it's so simple: the faithful are called to recognize their gifts and talents and use them for the service of others, and the Christian community is encouraged to call forth people with special gifts to use them for the common good. Translated into institutional terms, this means they use their gifts for the service of the church. Many Protestant churches have had this kind of official lay input for a long time.

While it is a great step forward for the Catholic Church, one side effect of a high level of lay involvement is that laypersons get a closer look at the church institution than they had ever had, and they are astonished by much of what they see. They see not only unlimited opportunities for helping other people, but also injustices, incompetence and insensitivity. They see that the church suffers from all of the shortcomings naturally associated with the human condition, and along with the positive development of a growing ecumenical understanding, they read and hear that their non-Catholic sisters and brothers experience the same kinds of problems. For many people, witnessing these flaws can be devastating. The wounds cut much deeper when people not only see the problems, but also experience them as their personal stake in the institution increases because of their greater involvement.

With a greater personal stake in the church, they also have a greater ownership of wounds. There are a greater number of hurt feelings, too, because as more people get involved in decision making, greater is the opportunity for disappointment when processes break down, which they frequently do.

Ed Wojcicki

If the church renovation committee chooses a design that I disagree with or the finance council votes not to spend money on saving the whales this year despite my brilliant position paper that took months to research, I am a candidate for disillusionment.

The church—clergy, vowed men and women, and laity—does not know yet what to do with this new problem. Certainly, church leaders and the hierarchy have a responsibility to respond. They have to learn more about what it means to be on the journey with the people of God instead of calling the shots from headquarters and assuming the people will go along. When there are wounds and hurt feelings, as there often are and always will be, church leaders have to learn to enter the healing process humbly. Church leaders, especially the clergy, who fail to do so, will quickly lose the trust of the people.

But that does not excuse the layperson from also having a humble role in the healing process. I try to be among the first people to say, "I don't expect the church to be perfect," but I also know that in my heart, I have very high expectations of the institutional church, to the point of tacitly imposing upon it the impossible requirements of being perfect in compassion, perfect in ministry, perfect in every way, especially in matters important to me.

That attitude is a setup for disillusionment, precisely because it is unfair. I want the church to be perfect, even though I cannot describe exactly what needs to happen or even what my own personal response should be.

What I do know is that the temptation to have an outlook

on life colored primarily by disillusionment and bitterness, although temporarily soothing in response to some difficult circumstances, is ultimately a poor choice as a way of life.

What is possible, instead, is hope.

Hope does not mean having a wish list and then hoping we get everything we want; nor does it mean that we should believe that without a doubt, improvement is probable in everything that is faulty in our personal lives and our daily routines and the institutions we belong to.

Hope, as I explain fully in the second section of this book, means that we live with the belief that something more fulfilling than a mere granting of our desires is possible in our lives. Something more deeply satisfying is possible. Something more meaningful is possible.

The person of hope learns a pace of life that at first may seem paradoxical. This pace is eternally trusting of God's movement in the world, and so there is patience. But it is also keenly sensitive to evils and human weakness, and so the person of hope is constantly moved to act with compassion. The person of hope is neither satisfied nor dissatisfied with the way things are.

Hope is a virtue open to everyone. This is a book about hope, focusing through many examples on why hope is possible in the places where most people spend most of their waking hours—at home, on the job, in community and school activities, and for many people, at church activities.

It is also about the obstacles to hope in our lives. The widow at Zarephath didn't think much of her handful of flour. And Jesus' staff of disciples must have been absolutely downcast when, with a hungry audience waiting, only five fish and two loaves of bread were on hand. With those few resources, however, Jesus fed 5,000 people!

I have learned that a handful of flour—that what I have and what is already available to me—is the handle on the door that shows me the way to a life of hope.

— Ed Wojcicki
Springfield, Illinois
March 1, 1991

NOTE TO INTRODUCTION

1. Ellen Goodman, "Across the country, middle class has the jitters," State Journal-Register, Springfield, Illinois; Oct. 3, 1990; page 5. (Goodman writes for the Boston Globe and syndicates her column.)

SECTION ONE

Obstacles and Challenges to Hope
in the Human Condition

CHAPTER ONE

Hopelessness at Many Stages of Life

A LL around us are invitations to hopelessness. Children, in their own immature way, sometimes believe that everybody is against them, and they get very sad. The adolescent, rattled by his or her own emotions, struggles incessantly with questions about self-esteem and intimacy. The young adult finds out how callous the world can be. The middle-aged person faces the major adjustment of wondering what to do with the startling realization that his or her ultimate dream can no longer be pursued. The older adult feels the temptation to say "What's the use?" because the second half of life is well under way, and older persons face the temptations of looking back with bitterness and giving in to a feeling that there is nothing left to do.

One of the most widely quoted affirmations of hopelessness is the Peter Principle, which states that "in a hierarchy every employee tends to rise to his level of incompetence."[1] In the Introduction to *The Peter Principle,* co-author Raymond Hull expresses his own version of hopelessness: "I have noticed that, with few exceptions, men bungle their affairs. Everywhere I see incompetence rampant, incompetence triumphant . . . I have accepted the universality of incompetence."[2] The book presses on relentlessly with the theory that going up the ladder until incompetence is achieved is an inescapable phenomenon.

31

Ed Wojcicki

I still remember that after working for only a few months as a newspaper reporter on my first job out of college, and seeing that neither my own company nor anything in the business world around me operated like a textbook operation, I called my dad and began to mutter and complain as if my discovery would amaze him. He interrupted me, though, after a short time and said just two things.

Without malice or anger or sarcasm, he stated, oh so matter-of-factly, "Son, you're beginning to learn what life is about," and then he threw out one of his favorite lines: "The first fifty years of working are the hardest." He also likes to say the first fifty years of marriage are the hardest.

How hard it was for me to have some of my youthful idealism and excitement chipped away. How hard it was, too, to realize that this kind of attitude adjustment is so normal and so natural that I should come to expect it!

At this stage of life, in one's early 20s, it is common to move toward settling down and finding a place in the adult world. It seems funny now, but at the time I graduated from high school, I thought I had just about everything figured out because I had grown up so much during that four-year period. Then a friend who graduated from college that same year told me I could expect to grow up that much more during my college years. I did not believe it was possible, because at no time other than at the age of eighteen, before or since, did I believe with such ignorant certainty that I understood life so well. I humbly learned in college that I knew very little about all there was to learn. The older I get, the more this trend continues: I learn every year that I know less and less.

32

A CRISIS OF HOPE

It was also a surprise to me when I discovered that the adulthood of age twenty-two is not the beginning of one, long, constant steady path. Adults continue to go through many phases of life, with ups and downs in every phase. "Our concentration during the Trying Twenties is on mastering what we feel we are *supposed* to do," award-winning journalist Gail Sheehy writes in the best-selling book, *Passages*. "The distinction is between the previous transition, the Pulling Up Roots years, when we knew what we *didn't want* to do, and the next transition, into the thirties, which will prod us toward doing what we *want* to do."[3]

Authors such as Sheehy, Erik Erikson and Daniel Levinson have become well-known for their efforts to identify these stages and the many changes that happen to adults even within each stage. Sheehy, describing a symposium called "Normal Crises of the Middle Years" in 1973, said the college auditorium "was packed with vague but hoping faces—an assortment, one imagined, of seekers, blamers, self-doubters, deserters, second and third marital offenders, abandoned middle-aged women, and fidgeting 'menopausal' males. All were anxious to hear what was normal about a crisis they had thought afflicted themselves alone."[4]

What I find significant about these studies is that a common theme running through adult lives at every stage is that everybody is searching for something. Everybody is searching for meaning. Everybody is searching for a niche in his or her community and in the world.

Depending on one's stage in life, the real or imagined object of the search will vary. The quality of the search will vary, and the intensity of the search will vary, too. What

33

does not change is that the search never ends. As an adult moves from one mini-stage to the next or successfully works through a crisis, new questions and new challenges emerge.

What also does not change is that with each stage and each challenge and each question, the possibility of losing hope is always one of the possible responses. Hope can be whittled away at any moment in any stage. High school graduates dream of reshaping the world according to the way they know it ought to be, but college graduates who do not land the perfect first job may begin to doubt their abilities. Young adults who get kicked around a bit on their first jobs begin to wonder if any company treats its employees with the highest of dignity. Most adults enter periods where their energy seems to run low and they begin to wonder whether they can keep up with their assorted responsibilities that include job, family and local community.

So many obstacles to hope jump into our lives frequently that, when we compare the bumpiness of life to the romantic notions of blissful joviality that we had conjured up in our younger days, it's no wonder that a sense of hopelessness begins to settle in. "Few people escape the fate that at one point or another in their development their hopes are disappointed—sometimes completely shattered . . . Hope is often shattered so thoroughly that a man may never recover it," German psychoanalyst Erich Fromm says.[5]

Fromm makes the important observation that hope is often badly misunderstood and that it has many imposters. What many people believe is hope is not hope at all but is actually a type of hopelessness.

A CRISIS OF HOPE

As a child I heard a slogan over again and again on television commercials: "To get a good job, get a good education." So I did—studied hard in high school in order to get into college, studied hard in college in order to land a job in my field, worked hard at the first job so that I would be in a position to get the next good job, and a better one after that.

Then it occurred to me one day that I was always living for the future. I was always living for whatever was supposed to happen next instead of getting the full enjoyment out of the present. I transferred the "to get a good job" mentality to most aspects of my life so thoroughly that an unfortunate byproduct was to ignore some current possibilities for friendships and enjoying life. I would shy away from immersing myself in community or church activities because, after all, I didn't expect to be in that community very long anyway. That was shortsighted, indeed, especially when I discovered I could have gone on like that without interruption—and someday I would be an eighty-five-year-old man who had never really lived.

So I am not saying it is wrong to get a good education or inappropriate to sacrifice anything today in order to put things in place for tomorrow. But Fromm correctly points out that a passive hope that amounts to a "worship of the future" is not hope at all, but the alienation of hope. He says in *The Revolution of Hope,* "Time and the future become the central category of this kind of hope. Nothing is expected to happen in the *now* but only in the next moment, the next day, the next year and in another world . . . Instead of something

35

Ed Wojcicki

I do or I become, the idols, future and posterity bring about something without my doing anything.'"[6]

Real hope, on the other hand, *shapes* our lives and our outlook on life. It is active, not passive, but not necessarily active in the sense of being busy or adventurous. Real hope is a way of being, a way of responding to life's challenges, and a way of positioning oneself in one's own circumstances. It must be nurtured consciously and frequently, because hope is easy to lose, and the ugly consequence of hopelessness is that all of our steam runs out. Hopelessness siphons our energy, and makes us cry out, "What's the use?"

Just as hope has imposters, such as a worship of the future, so, too, does hopelessness have many disguises—disguises that show up daily in the form of normal human emotions. Psychologists say we often fail to understand how to identify and deal with feelings such as anger, bitterness and frustration. We fail to see how these feelings chew us up and swallow our hope.

We need to understand that recognizing and identifying these feelings swirling within us are the first steps to recapturing a sense of active hope.

NOTES FROM CHAPTER ONE: HOPELESSNESS

1. Dr. Laurence J. Peter and Raymond Hull, *The Peter Principle* (New York: William Morrow & Company, Inc., 1969), 25.

2. *Ibid.,* 9, 11.

A CRISIS OF HOPE

3. Gail Sheehy, *Passages, Predictable Crises of Adult Life* (New York: E. P. Dutton & Co., Inc., 1976), 99.

4. *Ibid.*, 17.

5. Erich Fromm, *The Revolution of Hope* (New York: Harper & Row, 1968), 20.

6. *Ibid.*, 7.

CHAPTER TWO

Fear

PROBABLY most of us can remember being afraid as children. One of my earliest memories of being frightened was watching the movie *The Wizard of Oz*. I left the room and hid when the flying monkeys screeched and screamed on our black-and-white television set.

As far back as I can remember, I have also had a great fear of dogs. As a third grader with a paper route I did not want in the first place, I became terrified when the dogs started barking and especially when they roamed freely in the streets. My remedy then was to say a "Hail Mary" or to sing one of the hymns I had learned in the Catholic grade school. I imagine I was somewhat soothed by such prayerful remedies, and I don't remember being bit, either.

Fear is a basic human emotion, one that legitimately protects us from danger or harm. Children *should fear* crossing the street without carefully watching for cars, and adults *should fear* the consequences of walking too quickly on an icy sidewalk. To be afraid when one should be afraid is perfectly normal. Sometimes there is even a bit of humor in identifying the control that fears can have over people's lives. The five things most feared in a survey of 3,000 Americans were: speaking before a group; heights; insects and bugs; financial problems; and deep water. Thirteenth and fourteenth on the list were elevators and escalators, with elevators being slightly more feared.[1]

Herbert Fensterheim and Jean Baer have identified several basic kinds of fears.[2] The first is fairly obvious and lends itself to a list of "phobia" words—fears of things and places. For example, some people are deathly frightened by high places, a fear known as acrophobia; people who fear flying have aviaphobia; thunder, brontophobia; dogs, cynophobia; closed spaces, claustrophobia; night, nycotophobia; snakes, ophidiophobia; and so on.

Others don't dread things and places as much as they have interpersonal and social fears such as a fear of anger, tenderness, failure, success or rejection. "If you never take on a challenging task, you may never recognize that you fear failure," Fensterheim and Baer say. And "with most people, if things go wrong in a close relationship, they feel upset, unhappy and hurt but not destroyed. Life goes on. However, the person who is phobic of being hurt builds up the danger, does feel destroyed if it happens and takes fewer and fewer risks."[3]

We owe ourselves reasonable opportunities for personal growth and development. Sometimes this will require making sacrifices. If we go to college, for example, we usually postpone any major consumer binges. If we get married we henceforth have to consider our career choices in light of what's best for the whole family, not just for me. If we become a salesperson we realize that all of our time is not our own and we frequently must adjust personal schedules to meet the needs of customers.

Ed Wojcicki

What compounds every life decision is that fear is always waiting at the door. Fear, always a part of the internal conversations we have with ourselves, is anxious to strike a fatal blow to every idea that involves a risk. Fear is anxious to warn us to be cautious, sometimes overly cautious. When we give too much importance to such fears and settle for the easy way out, it becomes a way of life. We suddenly begin to hope for less. And in hoping for less, we gradually begin to believe that there is less to hope for, and the downward spiral toward hopelessness may become unstoppable.

This can happen in at least four major areas of our lives: in our careers, in relationships, in our local communities and in our spirituality.

I still remember one agonizing weekend after I was offered the job as editor of a small-town paper. At the time I felt quite secure and comfortable as the marketing director of the largest financial institution in our rural county. By switching jobs, I would be giving up the security of what I had, and I would be risking failure in becoming an editor for the first time. But with my journalism background and education, I knew in my heart that writing appealed to me much more than banking and marketing.

My wife and I discussed the offer at great length. I thought I should stay where I was and she thought I should go for the new challenge. Because of the stalemate—and we always talk over these big decisions—I quietly picked up my Bible and headed out to the city park, where I spent several hours walking, reading and reflecting. Those hours of prayer convinced me that I had been wrong and that I should accept the new job, but lo and behold, when I got home my wife had changed her mind, too, and we were again at a stalemate! To make a long story short, I called the publisher and asked for another day to think it over, and the next day I finally decided to make the switch from marketing to editing.

The biggest reason I considered not making the change was fear—fear of change and more likely than not, fear of failure and fear of the unknown. Fear almost caused me to cling to the security of what I had, even though it was already leading me toward professional stagnation when I was still in my 20s. How crafty fear can be in making complacency seem so appealing.

In careers, there is always the temptation to settle for where we are and thereby stop challenging ourselves. But we have to be careful, because there is a normal cycle of ups and downs on every job, and changing jobs every time a crisis occurs is not always the best answer. When major challenges occur on the job, fear usually tells us to run away, because the consequence of staying is to endure the pain that comes with dealing with a complex problem and working through it. (Anger, meanwhile, usually begs us to dream up schemes about heroically giving the boss a good chewing out, regardless of whether that's really a good idea.) Fear teaches us to avoid pain.

Hope in such circumstances, on the other hand, is anxious to remind us that something more deeply satisfying than the current level of security is always possible, too. Hope teaches us that pain and wounded feelings often are a necessary part of the process of growth and development as adults.

In relationships, very powerful fears and other emotions cause us to build walls that prevent intimacy. I still remember, with some pain, telling myself three years after moving to a new city that I could move out of that city and never return to visit anyone, because I had not developed any close relationships. It was the first time that had happened to me, and I finally admitted that I must have developed a fear of taking risks involved in establishing close, intimate friendships. I filled my waking hours with work, projects, chores, the sports page and television, and ignored the fact that building intimate friendships requires a major commitment of time. My marriage remained good and steady, but I secretly began to worry about what had happened to my ability to have close friends—the kind of friends I had had earlier in my life.

The title of John Powell's book, *Why Am I Afraid to Love?*, summarizes my point as well as anything.[4] A fear of intimacy is probably accompanied by a loss of hope, because without movement toward intimacy, the void is filled with a deep loneliness that causes people to wonder whether there is any reason to hope.

In our communities, fear also plays a role in stopping us from getting as involved as we should. Fear of failure and fear of rejection become common reasons for not doing something that would be terrific for the community. Even the biggest ideas are often born from a simple hunch. How much different would history be, for example, if the Wright brothers had not gone to the sandy, windy beaches of North Carolina near Kitty Hawk to test their idea of a flying machine? And how much poorer might the United States be in the preservation of its heritage if James Smithson, a European who never even set foot on North American soil, had not bequeathed his 19th century fortune to the young United States for the "increase and diffusion of knowledge among men"? His fortune provided the base for the Smithsonian Institution.

On the other hand, we will never know how many great ideas have died in the secrets of people's hearts for lack of response by those who dismissed their brilliant ideas as impossible dreams. I wonder how many people, especially in smaller communities, have dreamed of being involved in projects where the arts or music or literature would flourish, only to have their dream die quickly due primarily to fear of failure. How much we admire, though, the person who becomes the champion of a bold new idea and carries the banner despite a dragging of the feet by doomsayers. Certainly people like Cesar Chavez of the migrant workers feared failure, embarrassment and rejection on many occasions, but stuck with the cause for the sake of the common good.

No matter whether a project is small or major, the same emotional risks are involved. At meetings we attend, how often we see good ideas set aside because not one person is willing to take the risk of overcoming the obstacles that everyone knows will get in the way of implementing them. The most common objection is that not enough people will rally behind the effort, and therefore, the idea dies. I will deal with this kind of apathy more thoroughly in a later chapter. It is not possible, of course, to take up every good idea. But it is energizing to wonder how much better off our communities would be if a few more people became the champions of a few more good ideas. My concern is that the more comfortable we get with rejecting good ideas quickly, even for "reasonable" causes, the more likely it is that as a community we will settle flatly for the status quo and lose the kind of hope that gives us a vision of something more fulfilling.

Finally, in our spirituality, fear is a major cause of settling for what we already have. By using the word spirituality in this context, I am using its broadest possible definition to include all of the various feelings and emotions and reflections that swirl around within us, often unconsciously and often in ways known only to ourselves. People commonly fear the consequences of dealing honestly with these "spiritual" nudgings, even in rather simple matters such as deciding whether to blow the whistle when they see co-workers stealing from the company or friends cheating on their spouses. In either case they fear getting people upset with them; so the safer course is to say nothing.

At another level of spirituality, people fear that a conversion or a deeper conversion to God will lead them away from the things they enjoy most in life, such as recreation, the comforts of life and good times. They fear losing control over their lives, especially if they are aware of Jesus' warning that his aim is to comfort the afflicted and afflict the comfortable.

The Scriptures are full of examples of God's favorite people demonstrating for all future generations just how afraid they were, and the inhibiting consequences of being so full of fear. But the Bible overflows with different ways, throughout the Old and New Testaments, that God tells his followers they need not be afraid if they trust in him. How often he and his prophetic messengers try to comfort us with pleas to "fear not" and "be not afraid." This was the message from angels at the triumphant moments of Jesus' birth and resurrection. This is the message from Isaiah: "Fear not, I am with you; be not dismayed; I am your God. I will strengthen you and help you, and uphold you with my right hand of justice" (*Isaiah* 41:10). Remember what the gospel writer Matthew recorded as Jesus' first words to his disciples after the resurrection: "Do not be afraid . . ." (*Matthew* 28:10).

One reason the Bible is full of references to fear must be that fear is one of the most significant obstacles to a deeper spiritual life for most people. In praying and reading the Scriptures, I constantly find God coaxing me to a deeper belief in him. But I also catch myself rejecting his welcoming hand, because I fear he might be calling me where I would rather not go. I still nourish and cling to unsettling fears about how my life would change if I trusted God totally instead of allocating most of my time to job security, my ability to figure things out, and my ongoing concerns for a comfortable house, good food and a reasonably good car.

This kind of fear does not necessarily paralyze us or drive us to inaction, but it does quietly deceive us into becoming comfortable with where we are and what we have. Such fear of risk-taking causes us to have less hope, because in becoming too satisfied we teach ourselves to ignore our innermost desire for something more fulfilling.

We should have a fear of being too comfortable, because complacency is an enemy of hope.

Ed Wojcicki

NOTES TO CHAPTER 2: FEAR

1. David Wallechinsky, Irving Wallace and Amy Wallace, *The Book of Lists* (New York: Bantam Books, Inc., 1977), 469-470, as reported in the *Sunday Times* of London, Oct. 7, 1973.

2. Herbert Fensterheim, Ph.D., and Jean Baer, *Stop Running Scared* (New York: Rawson Associates Publishers, Inc., 1977), 31-33.

3. *Ibid.*, 32.

4. John Powell, S.J., *Why Am I Afraid to Love?* (Chicago: Argus Communications, 1967).

CHAPTER THREE

Anger

I was angry with my friends;
I told my wrath, my wrath did end.
I was angry with my foe;
I told it not, my wrath did grow.
                    —William Blake

OF ALL the human emotions and reactions, anger is a favorite among psychologists. Like fear, anger is a natural human response. Anger is an intense, reactive emotion that is stirred up when a person perceives that emotional or physical injury has been done to oneself or others.

Since the prevailing popular American attitude seems to be that anger is mostly negative and a sign that somebody is out of control, it's important to say up front that anger itself is not a problem; what matters is how we respond to it. Anger induces emotional and biochemical responses in the body. Dr. James Dobson, head of the California-based Focus on the Family and author of *Emotions: Can You Trust Them,* explains in easy-to-understand language just how natural the biochemical response is:

This is an involuntary response which occurs whether or not we will it. All anger produces biochemical changes in the body, although the hormones released through irri-

Ed Wojcicki

tating circumstances are somewhat different from the fight or flight system, [which kicks on when people feel provoked or threatened]. I might also say that each individual has his own unique pattern of responses. Some people become overheated with the slightest provocation, and others are cool characters who seem to be born with an ability to stay above it all. These differences are partially hereditary and partially conditioned by environmental circumstances during and after childhood.[1]

In response to anger, people typically respond in one of several basic ways:

—With violence: by harming individuals or things with physical or verbal abuse.
—With repression: by underreacting, and without realizing it, pushing anger inward and letting it simmer. This "is psychologically hazardous," Dobson says. "The pressure that it generates will usually appear elsewhere in the form of depression, anxiety, tension, or an entire range of physical disorders."[2]
—With suppression: by blocking out or denying the anger, in a more conscious manner than repression.
—With silence or superficial indifference: by not dealing with what makes them angry and thereby deceiving themselves into believing this is coolheaded, mature and healthy.
—In positive ways: by "releasing" the anger in conversations or activity that is not abusive of themselves or others. Psychologists generally refer to this kind of response as quite healthy.

48

A CRISIS OF HOPE

John Powers, author of *Mirror, Mirror on the Wall: The Art of Talking With Yourself,* sums it up well by saying that anger can be a personal friend or personal enemy. Anger, he says, "is one of the most powerful, complex, stimulating and creative emotions; yet it is also the most potentially destructive . . . Whether your anger is friend or foe depends to a large degree upon your respect for this necessary human emotion and whether your anger flows from love or is born of resentful hurt."[3]

APPROPRIATE ANGER

Perhaps an example will help explain what I mean. Encountering anger is like approaching a closed door with a neutral sign that says, simply, "Anger." When we arrive at the door, we have three choices. One is to walk away and avoid the encounter, without realizing that whatever path we take will either lead us to this door once again, or to a back door from which the anger will deal with us before we deal with it. A second choice is to pound mightily on the door until we either break a hand or knock a hole in the door. The third choice is to knock politely, and when the door is opened, to ask if we can enter and discuss what is behind the angry door. Sometimes we will find another person there and engage in conversation to explore the anger; other times we might remain alone to reflect on the anger in a quiet place.

There is a big difference between responding appropriately in anger to a specific situation and living in a state of perpetual anger. There is much to be angry about in our imperfect

49

world. We should feel anger when a co-worker consistently goofs up, making our own working environment more inefficient. We should be angry when fellow employees are treated inhumanely or are the victims of incompetence, harassment or ignorance in the workplace. We should be angry when political decisions are the causes of hunger, suffering or death for millions of our sisters and brothers who share the planet. We should be angry when someone begins to abuse us or takes advantage of us, or when we find out that someone is bad-mouthing us behind our backs. We should be angry when we find that a store clerk has sold us a defective product intentionally, or deliberately given us the wrong merchandise. We should be angry when our children blatantly disobey us.

Even though not all of these examples have major significance in our lives, all are legitimate causes for anger, and it's important to be able to say that. To be angry in such circumstances is normal and even necessary, for anger whose cause is known and identified can stimulate us to take positive steps to address the problems.

WHEN ANGER IS AN ENEMY OF HOPE

To *refuse* to deal with anger, on the other hand, can cause people to release their anger wildly and unconsciously at targets unrelated to the source of their pain. How sad it is to listen to a person for whom nothing ever goes right and who feels like a victim of all of his or her life's circumstances. Such a person finds major fault with just about everything—from job to family to friends to the supermarket clerk. The person may be very angry about only one area of his or her life, but an inability to deal with it causes the anger to spill over into every other aspect of life. Chronically angry people are not always, and perhaps not often, aware that they are so angry or why they are angry, although they know they don't feel very happy. Sometimes, psychologists say, the lingering anger is connected to an event long ago in life, perhaps in childhood, but the anger has been pushed down for many years.

Left unattended, anger can seriously deteriorate one's emotions and lead to frustration, disillusionment, self-righteousness, depression, violence, bitterness, apathy or cynicism—or perhaps all of them. I will deal with these topics at greater length in other chapters, but just listing them here gives a good indication of why anger is a major concern of therapists. It also is well-known that anger left unattended can lead to serious physical problems, such as heart disease.

Anger, as the fertilizer for numerous emotional and physical illnesses, is probably the number one enemy of hope, because it can impede one's ability to hope for something more deeply satisfying in life. The person who is angry about life—period—develops an outlook that perceives hope only as a virtue of fools.

According to family therapist Martin Padovani, "If we do not deal with the anger that we feel, our relationships lead to resentment, bitterness, and hostility. You can see this in problem families and in troubled marriages. In the latter, the anger is frequently connected with extra-marital affairs. A large percent of extra-marital affairs have some element of anger in them . . . The amount of destructiveness and agony that occurs in people's lives because anger is not recognized and appropriately dealt with is beyond our comprehension.''[4]

When anger is not dealt with, it impedes hope because anger never simply goes away all by itself. Where anger prevails, hope will always be on the periphery; because anger first *requires a response* to perceived emotional or physical injury, and hope is a virtue that looks beyond injury and insists that something more deeply satisfying is possible.

''More marriages and families today are dying from silence than from violence,'' Padovani asserts. ''In nine out of ten marriages I deal with, this is the situation. Silence. Repressed anger. Unexpected hostility. Coldness. All are devious and unhealthy ways by which people get back at each other.''[5]

A SPECIFIC EXAMPLE—ANGER IN THE CHURCH

Anger, as a natural human emotion, does not exempt itself from any place where people live and work—not from families, not from businesses, and not from churches. While organized religion from a distance generally enjoys a reputation as helping, consoling and nourishing peoples' lives, in the internal structures can be found many ministers, laypersons and leaders seething with anger related to the institution itself. The kind of infighting that is found universally in social, economic and political organizations is also evident in the church. It is not hard to find ministers who are angry with their congregations, their superiors, their fellow ministers, or with themselves. And church members regularly become angry with their pastors and with each other, sometimes for "material" reasons such as the raising of funds for a new church, but often for other reasons such as the minister's style of leadership. Factionalism is common.

Is it possible for organized religion, rampant with angry people, also to be a witness of hope for the world? Again I must distinguish between anger directed at a specific situation and a general state of anger, and repeat that even where there is a lot of anger, the problem is not so much the anger as how people respond to it. And here I will make a third distinction: it is important *not* to conclude that an entire industry or institution is angry just because some of its members or some of its leaders are angry.

In the Catholic Church in the United States, one prominent issue fueled by plenty of anger revolves around how women have been and are treated in a traditional, male-led institution. Part of this debate revolves around what roles women ought to have, because the Catholic Church prohibits the ordination of women as bishops, priests and deacons. But far more significant are numerous concerns related to how women feel in an organization in which, no matter how enlightened or educated, they still usually have to answer to a clergy*man*.

Because this is such a hot topic, Catholic bishops in the U.S. spent several years in the late 1980s formally soliciting the viewpoints of thousands of people, especially women, in preparation for writing a pastoral letter from all of the bishops to all U.S. Catholics on women-related issues. The first draft of the bishops' lengthy letter, released in 1988 and later revised after much public discussion, included several sections entitled "Listening to the Voices of Alienation" and acknowledged how much anger is stored up in the church. At one point the bishops wrote:

> Admittedly, women are frustrated when they are prevented from assuming roles officially open in the church but locally closed off by clerical leaders who hold to old stereotypes. Such attitudes affect not only women's opportunities in ministry but their spiritual growth as well.
>
> [Quoting from an official report from the Diocese of Joliet, Ill.] "The spiritual lives of women have been regulated and legislated almost exclusively by males, with clergy measuring women's virtue and spiritual growth against the standards of a male perspective. Often, too, double standards for men and women have been operative in the areas of morality as well as spirituality."
>
> Some women have been alienated from the church by attitudes which assume they are not to assert themselves, but to remain in assigned and secondary places. Women believe it is time to re-examine the sources of these attitudes and to work together to create mutuality and foster renewal.[6]

The women who have responded to their anger by challenging church leaders to re-evaluate their attitudes and decisions have done a great service for the church, and have found a most positive way of dealing with their anger. They should be admired for expressing their concerns, because they know the issues are complex and that not all women in the church share their feelings of second-class treatment. This Catholic debate has been so lively that it is tempting for me to delve into the subject further and further. But such a digression could not be accomplished without a thorough historical analysis of women's roles in society in general—and how much these have changed just in the past generation. So I will move on, very much encouraged by the fact that in the Catholic Church a discussion about "women's concerns" is being conducted publicly and with high visibility, rather than informally and only in unofficial circles where women (and men who share their concerns) would believe there is no way that airing their concerns would make a difference.

ANGER AND HOPE

Is it possible, then, to be angry and hopeful at the same time? Yes, because anger can be a specific, appropriate response to a particular situation, and both *dealing with anger* and *being a person of hope* involve personal processes that require plenty of time to work out. Many occurrences can provoke anger, and just because one becomes angry for a while does not mean that hope has been abandoned. Anger, while described earlier as hope's number one enemy, can also, paradoxically enough, be an *agent of hope* when it is part of the process that leads to our growth and development; that is, when it contributes to our understanding that something more deeply satisfying in life is possible. As Padovani says:

Anger is absolutely necessary for mature human relationships! The more intimate I am with you, the more necessary it is for us to be open with each other. And this will sometimes mean showing our anger with each other.

But we are afraid of doing this. Why? Because we feel we shall hurt each other. But if we are going to be honest with each other, we are going to hurt each other.[7]

The idea, of course, is not to make plans to hurt each other, but to recognize anger for what it is and use it as an opportunity for understanding each other better. Expressing a desire to identify and deal with anger can itself be a sign of hope. Mixing hope with an emotion like fear or anger can give us a sense of courage. With courage and hope, we more readily see the value of dealing with anger positively and appropriately. John Powers says we should be willing to make anger a personal friend:

> Befriending your anger is a liberating process. If you have ignored, buried or repressed powerful angry feelings, they have become a foe you will one day have to reckon with in crisis. But if you are able to name your angry feelings, name the cause of the object of your anger, purify your motives, uncover hidden anger, [and] express your anger appropriately and positively, then there is the possibility of inner serenity.[8]

One note of caution about dealing positively with anger: we always have to recognize whether and to what extent we can be an agent of change. If we are angry at a situation, can we realistically change anything when we deal with it? If we are angry at another person, can we really change that person's attitude or behavior?

I respond to these questions at two levels: an ideal level and a more practical level. For example, if we are angry about the existence of war and terrorism, we must realize that we are setting ourselves up for disappointment at the idealistic level if we set a goal of achieving peace on earth within ten years, or within our lifetime, for that matter. Similarly, if we are angry that our place of employment is far from a text-book example of proper concern for employees, we set ourselves up for failure if we believe we can perfect the system. No human system can be perfected, and it's even rare that a Martin Luther King Jr. comes along with the charisma, ability and perseverance to bend the conscience of an entire nation about an issue that makes most people angry.

But when our anger causes us to ask whether we can be an agent of change, we should recognize that often there are some reasonable, practical steps we can take. The change may not take place exactly as we had hoped or as fast as it should, or it might not take place at all, but at least we will have dealt with our anger in a positive way and perhaps even affected the source of the anger.

Dr. Dobson points out that sometimes we must admit that there is actually very little we can do to change the circumstances that cause our anger. One time he laid this out bluntly to a woman whose father had had a difficult childhood himself and who never showed his daughter any signs of love. Dobson wrote her in a letter:

. . . Your dad never met the needs that a father should satisfy in his little girl, and I think you are still hoping he will miraculously become what he has never been. Therefore, he constantly disappoints you—hurts you—rejects you. I think you will be less vulnerable to pain when you accept the fact that he cannot, nor will he ever, provide the love and empathy and interest that he should. It is not easy to insulate yourself in this way. I'm still working to plug a few vacuums from my own tender years. But it hurts less to expect nothing than to hope in vain.[9]

To live in expectation of nothing in such painful circumstances is not the same thing as living in hopelessness. The *most practical, realistic* response to some situations is to lower our expectations so much that we seriously doubt that improvement or "something better" is possible. While this is reasonable in some circumstances, it is not the same thing as saying there is no longer reason to hope that "something more fulfilling" is possible for us in life. As I will explain more fully in the second section of this book, there is a significant difference between wanting something to be better and hoping for something more deeply satisfying.

Learning to deal with anger courageously, hopefully and positively will be a lifetime challenge for most of us, for there is always more to learn as life presents us with new challenges. With hope, over a period of time, we can learn to make anger an ally in some significantly mature ways:

—By talking it over with a third party unrelated to the source of anger, without harming the reputation of anyone.

—By distinguishing honestly between when anger is justifiable as a normal response and when our response is inappropriate because it's harmful to myself or others. For some reason I get very, very angry, for example, when someone cuts me off while driving on a busy city street, but all too commonly I respond by honking wildly or tailgating the one who has offended me. This is clearly inappropriate and juvenile.

—By expressing to others, without being vicious or vengeful or overly accusatory, that we feel angry after they did or said something.

—By recognizing that while we cannot always stop, nor should we want to stop, the physiological processes connected with anger, we can choose how we will respond.

—By welcoming the anger and recognizing its benefits. "Even if we feel rage, even if we feel like tearing someone apart, these are only feelings," Padovani says. "We have to allow ourselves to be angry with God, our church, our spouse, our children, our parents—dead or alive."[10]

And then we must respond as immediately as circumstances allow, as intelligently as the circumstances permit, and with as much hope and courage as we can muster.

NOTES TO CHAPTER 3: ANGER

1. Dr. James Dobson, *Emotions, Can You Trust Them?* (Ventura, California: Regal Books, 1980), 86-87.

2. *Ibid.,* 93.

3. John Powers, *Mirror Mirror on the Wall: The Art of Talking With Yourself* (Mystic, CT: Twenty-Third Publications, 1987), 18-19.

4. Martin H. Padovani, *Healing Wounded Emotions: Overcoming Life's Hurts* (Mystic, CT, D6355-0180: Twenty-Third Publications, 1987), 27-28.

5. *Ibid.,* 30.

6. U.S. Catholic Conference, *Partners in the Mystery of Redemption: A Pastoral Response to Women's Concerns for Church and Society* (Washington, D.C., 1988), paragraphs 186-187. At the time of this writing a second draft of the pastoral letter was already complete; but a date for a vote by the bishops on a final draft was still not known.

7. Padovani, *Healing Wounded Emotions*, 28.

8. Powers, *Mirror, Mirror on the Wall*, 23.

9. *Dr. James Dobson, What Wives Wish Their Husbands Knew About Women* (Wheaton, Illinois: Tyndale House Publishers, 1975), 181-183.

10. Padovani, *Healing Wounded Emotions*, 32.

CHAPTER FOUR

Self-Righteousness, Mistakes and Impatience

I'VE BEEN an editor at three different newspapers, and at two of them I started a program that taught me a lot about readers and about people in general. Once a year, I invited everybody who had had letters to the editor published in the previous year to a free lunch. Some of them, of course, had accused me of idiocy and not doing my job very well, while a significant but smaller number had complimented my work. Some had also written to explain why other letter writers had a few screws loose.

The "program" after the luncheons was simple to design: just open the floor to a discussion about the newspaper and current issues. The discussion always got interesting very quickly, and intermittently became quite heated. As moderator of the discussion, I attempted to give everyone a chance to say something, and I'd occasionally hear low-volume sneers from one part of the room while someone else was speaking. An attitude of active listening helped me in one important way: usually after someone rose to criticize me, someone else rose to defend me before I could respond.

These luncheons indelibly imprinted on me the value of patient listening. Even people with whom I disagreed strongly generally had some truths or valid insights in their statements. By listening patiently and processing the other's thought rather than anxiously waiting to retort, I have discovered, first of all, that most issues have not just two but many sides, and secondly, that my own point of view usually has its own inconsistencies that I need to examine. Over a period of months or years, as I continually listen and process new information, I now find it not so difficult to admit my own errors, to change my opinion, and—gulp!—to see wisdom in opinions I once considered foolish.

In my first few jobs, for example, as a person far down on the organizational chart, I remember how easy it was to criticize the boss. How commonly employees in most places grumble about management style or specific management decisions, and how commonly the words flow, ''If I were boss . . .'' Yes, if I were boss, things would be done right! Things would be done differently! Profits and percentages would not be preached to the employees, because what matters most is paying attention to the needs of the workers! Don't they see that if they would pay me and the other good employees just a little more, we'd gladly stay around and thereby improve their bottom line! Don't buy all that expensive equipment—just pay me a little more instead!

Then one day I became the boss, where I saw rather quickly that life would be more complicated. I appreciated the management training programs that taught me more about active listening to employees and collaborating with them so that as many decisions as possible would be made with their input, but I also realized that some decisions that had to be made would be unpopular. I also understood for the first time that it was literally impossible to keep the organization going without having a surplus (sometimes known as profit) and having a little financial cushion for expansion and major purchases.

I began to learn the difference between being right and being self-righteous. Being right requires some kind of factual basis for proving indisputably that my understanding, belief or opinion is correct and that I could not possibly be wrong. Being self-righteous, on the other hand, is to *place myself* arrogantly on higher moral ground or on a level of higher principles than others, thereby making me "right" principly because I perceive myself as more principled than anybody who disagrees with me. If I am self-righteous and others take issue with me, I can shoot them down immediately by saying they simply do not understand the big picture. Self-righteous people have a habit of being obnoxious. It's easy to root against self-righteous people.

That's why it became a national pastime to poke fun at Richard Nixon in the mid-1970s. He had dug himself into a deep hole by insisting that he had done nothing wrong and had taken no part in discussions about covering up activity related to the Watergate break-in. His stubbornness and self-righteousness got the best of him, and the public responded with disdain. Similarly, television preacher Jimmy Swaggart rankled many people as he built a national reputation in the 1980s by preaching against sin and condemning many long-standing Christian denominations for not being as close to the pure truth as he was. Then he got caught in a sex scandal, and continued to dig in his heels by refusing to accept the recommended punishment—suspension as a preacher—by his own denomination, the Assemblies of God.

Ed Wojcicki

Most people have a little self-righteousness in them. They dig in on some issues, some beliefs, and some personal habits, and they won't budge. They won't relinquish their opinion that Nixon was a very good president; they won't budge from their deeply held prejudice that they could never have a woman for a boss, or, citing smokers' rights, they refuse to quit smoking in small closed rooms despite the objections of others. Such attitudes make it difficult to have hope if we dig in to such a point that we perceive others or the world itself as pitted against us in a very personal way, or when we set ourselves up in self-righteous conflict with others. We create a setting in which we have pronounced the truth and drawn the line, and we stand, arms akimbo, by the line and dare somebody to cross it. It's as if we say: Don't ask a question and don't disagree and don't cross the line. And then we lose hope because we were foolish in the first place, to believe that everybody is going to be in accord with our perspective.

This is true not only in one-on-one relationships but also in groups. How often I have listened at meetings to discussions about a problem, and sat there smugly, knowing I had *the* perfect solution. I waited for the dramatic moment, expressed my opinion (sometimes stumbling over my words in the process), and then watched in embarrassment as the group dismissed my idea or glossed over it as irrelevant. My smugness disappears instantly when I realize, either while hearing my own words, or by the reaction of indifference, that I didn't have the solution after all.

Most of us are intelligent enough to say we do not have all the answers, but too often we act as if we have more answers than we really do. Pride sets in, and pride breeds bitterness. Feeling we are right to a relentless degree causes us to do great damage to others. We cause divisions. We gossip. We plot. We create scapegoats. We blame the boss, or we blame the employees. We blame the spouse. We blame the kids. We blame the parents. Or the minister. We blame the coach, the umpire, the teacher, or society. Or the Republicans. And we talk negatively about them with all of the harshness and incredulity that we can muster. Because we are right, by golly, we want everybody else to see it our way and do it our way. Sometimes the consequences are not only harmful, but tragic.

Consider the "fatal flaw" found in the great literary tragedies. A fatal flaw is a dominant negative characteristic in a person that leads to his or her downfall. The tragedy in these stories is that a person cannot recognize or deal with the flaw in a healthy manner—hence the term, fatal flaw.

In Nathaniel Hawthorne's *The Birthmark,* a brilliant scientist named Aylmer married a beautiful woman named Georgiana, who had on one cheek a tiny crimson birthmark the shape roughly of a small human hand. The woman was so beautiful that most men could overlook her small blemish. But Aylmer became preoccupied with it and eventually repulsed by it. So with his scientific genius he concocted for Georgiana a medicinal drink to make the birthmark go away. It worked, but just as the last tint of crimson faded, Georgiana died from consuming the beverage. Aylmer's pride in his scientific ability, coupled by a relentless disdain for one small flaw in his wife's appearance, caused him to misplace his priorities totally, and to kill his wife.[1]

65

Ed Wojcicki

By his intolerance of what he foolishly perceived as a problem on his wife's cheek, Aylmer prevented himself from having hope for a happy future. How ironic that in the human race where flaws and mistakes are so common that we should naturally expect them to happen, impatience with mistakes and intolerance of flaws are among our greatest obstacles to hope. How unfortunate that although we know mistakes will happen and problems occur, we so frequently respond to them by saying, "It should not have happened then" or "He sure picked the wrong time to make a mistake." We should ask ourselves: When *is* the right time to make a mistake?

I think about this often while watching children play sports. Even for children six years old or younger, adults establish athletic organizations and competition, and then sit along the sidelines to watch the exciting action. More often than I would like to admit, I have to stop myself from reacting to a bad play as if the kids were adult professionals. I have to remind myself that they are only children—very young children, in fact—and when I was a kid, nobody was scouting me for a major college scholarship, either! Meanwhile, some of the kids just beyond the toddler stage forget where they are during the game because their attention span isn't long enough. Showing up for an organized contest is simply another part of a day of playing for them. They ask about the score, but seem just as interested in the treats after the game, while *the parents* concern themselves with who won and who lost. My wife loves to ask the question: "If it doesn't matter who wins then why do they keep score?"

A CRISIS OF HOPE

We ought to have the patience to really accept that not only will we make mistakes, but so will everybody else. Mistakes are actually good for us as long as we learn from them. Tom Peters, author of several books in the 1980s about management practices in business, believes that mistakes should be not only tolerated, but encouraged. In *A Passion for Excellence,* he and co-author Nancy Austin explain that mistakes are a necessary part of testing new ideas, and that testing and failing are necessary if any improvement is to be realized. "To test is to fail, repeatedly," they say.[2]

They advance that idea many steps, in fact, by declaring that companies should talk about their failures, tell stories about their failures, and practically celebrate when the "good try" fails. They carefully distinguish between a sloppy effort and a legitimate good try. But they just as emphatically insist that admitting mistakes and making mistakes is an essential part of learning, and that too many people attempt to hide mistakes or cover them up instead of learning from them. Among the sorry rationalizations they have commonly found are organizations where not enough homage is paid to innovative trying and failing:

(1) A "good presentation" counts as much as a report of concrete action, (2) good logic and lots of data substitute for action, (3) the explanation that it couldn't get done because of budget or an inability to get certain people or departments together is considered adequate as long as there is "evidence" demonstrating that "we" tried and "they" were recalcitrant, (4) you "need more staff work," or "need more expensive data" or "should form a commit-

tee'' (the typical disposition of nine out of ten agenda items at the department, division, corporate or board level). It all adds up to trappings and audit trails being more important than doing . . . It isn't pretty.[3]

Having a balanced response to mistakes, errors and weaknesses in others cuts off the emotional need to be self-righteous. It prevents us from having a need to see ourselves as right and others wrong or less principled. It allows us and those around us more freedom to make mistakes, and hence, the freedom to dream and grow and develop.

Going through periods of self-righteousness—believing with all earnestness that we could not possibly be wrong—is as normal as the daily sunrise. The really big trouble begins when a person never learns that being wrong is not such a bad thing. The chronically self-righteous person is destined for disillusionment and bitterness. This will become more clear when I discuss Phil Donahue's autobiography in the chapter on cynicism.

The flip side of this entire discussion about impatience and self-righteousness, of course, is that sometimes the stubborn, relentless person with an unpopular, grating message really is right. Society needs people living on the edge of change; it needs prophets calling the rest of us to a higher ground, not only regarding the great social issues but also in more common places such as in every home and in every place of business. We know from history that today's audacious statements sometimes become tomorrow's wisdom. Martin Luther King Jr., assassinated in 1968, is now almost universally accepted as a civil rights prophet of the 1950s and 1960s,

A CRISIS OF HOPE

whereas during his lifetime he had uttered many "hard sayings" that people found difficult to swallow.

The trouble with discerning prophetic voices, especially if we wonder whether we ourselves are in such a role, is that it is nearly impossible to know at the present moment whether an idea is truly prophetic, merely trendy, or actually misleading—although seemingly plausible at the time. Sometimes it turns out that we were right all along. Other times we believed we had all the facts when we really did not. The cliche tells us there are two sides to every story, but in reality, there are always many sides with many nuances in every conflict. There are usually as many sides as there are people involved, and usually every side contains at least a bit of the truth.

So the first person I distrust is one who tells me he or she is absolutely certain of his or her opinion about a complex issue or a complex personality. The second person I have learned to take with a grain of salt is myself, especially when I get on a roll about something and I become determined to prove how correct I am. As Jawaharlal Nehru once said:

> Let us be a little humble; let us think that the truth may not perhaps be entirely with us. Let us cooperate with others; let us, even when we do not appreciate what others say, respect their views and their ways of life.[4]

Similarly, the eighteenth century Swiss philosopher Johann Georg von Zimmermann issued some good advice when he said, "Humility is the first lesson we learn from reflection, and self-distrust the first proof we give of having obtained a knowledge of ourselves."[5]

Ed Wojcicki

Humility is the best preventive medicine and the best remedy for pride, self-righteousness and impatience. Without humility there can be no hope, for if we believe only in ourselves, we can have no hope of anything more deeply satisfying in life. We might as well face up to what we already know: there is no chance that the rest of the world will conform to our limited view of the way things ought to be. Our personal frame of reference is by definition limited, making it essential always to live as if we are not too certain that we are right.

NOTES TO CHAPTER FOUR: SELF-RIGHTEOUSNESS, MISTAKES AND IMPATIENCE

1. Nathaniel Hawthorne, ''The Birthmark,'' in *The Norton Anthology of Short Fiction* (New York: W. W. Norton & Company, Second Edition, 1981), 600-613.

2. Tom Peters and Nancy Austin, *A Passion for Excellence* (New York: Random House, 1985), 180.

3. *Ibid.,* 181-182.

4. John P. Bradley, Leo F. Daniels, and Thomas C. Jones, *The International Encyclopedia of Quotations* (Chicago: J.G. Ferguson Publishing Company, 1978), 371.

5. *Ibid.*

CHAPTER FIVE

Frustration

K ITTY SCANLAN finds plenty of reasons for frustration in her job as an occupational therapist. As told to Studs Terkel in his book *Working,* she explains:

Until recently, I wasn't sure how meaningful my work was. I had doubts. A surgeon does a really beautiful job. That's meaningful to him *immediately.* But it's not the kind of sustaining thing that makes a job meaningful. It must concern the relationship you have with the people you work with. We get hung up on the competition . . .

That's what happens in hospitals—not because people are unfeeling or don't care, but because they feel put down. You have to protect yourself in some way. Many things in the institution frustrate me. The doctor who refuses to deal with the patient who knows he's dying. He says, "He doesn't want to know anything." Or the alcoholic with cirrhosis. What's the use of putting him in this hospital bed, prolonging his life, to send him back to the lonely, isolated world where he'll sit in his room and drink and nobody to cook for him? You know there's no place to send him. Or the old lady who's had a stroke, and lives alone . . . And the bastards you have to deal with—sarcastic doctors. They're not really bastards—it's the way the institution makes them. You think, "What's the use?"[1]

Ed Wojcicki

There is no more useful definition of frustration than that of a person sighing slowly and saying, "What's the use?"

Many people, like Kitty Scanlan, feel frustrated on the job. I once worked for a company that, on paper, encouraged us to think about what new products our company might make. So I went to my supervisor with three ideas. A few days later, he told me that the corporate policy is for me to use "my own resources" to do all of the research and investigation, and that if I could prove the product would make money, submit the idea. How ridiculous! How discouraging that I was not allowed to make even a single long-distance phone call to test an idea that eventually could make the company more profitable. If I could prove, with all of my own resources, that something could make money, why wouldn't I go to the bank and borrow the money and keep all the profit myself? Frustrated by the response, I pursued none of the ideas further (I had no resources) and I never submitted another idea.

Being frustrated, like getting angry, is a fact of life not only on the job but in nearly every aspect of our lives. Being frustrated is a step beyond being disappointed. We are disappointed when our favorite sports team loses a game. We are disappointed when we go to the car dealer and find out the car we really want is one or two price ranges beyond our ability to pay. We are disappointed when the "creeping Charlie" strangles our lawn three summers in a row. But rarely are these the kinds of issues that send us into despair.

Frustration is usually longer in duration than disappointment, and often the result not of one major negative experience, but a series of small bad experiences interconnected in some way. Frustration on the job, for example, does not settle in on the first day, when optimism runs high and often there is excitement about a new venture. No, frustration enters only after discovering the co-worker across the aisle gabs too much, more and more customers are preparing to go to the competition, and the boss has such an ego that one of your duties is to listen to stories about his heroics every day. Only gradually do such details wear you down and get you frustrated and you discover you no longer know how to respond.

Once this happens, whether at work, at home or elsewhere in our lives, we often summarize or even blame our frustration on a single dramatic incident, even though a more objective analysis would tell us that the frustration had been building, and what we blame on the single incident is not really the major issue in our lives.

When my first child was a toddler, our church had no crying room or parents' room. So we regularly sat in the choir loft in the back of the church to give our daughter some room to spread out and not bother anyone. One morning, when we were in the front row of the choir loft, the pastor chose that Sunday to explain why he would, in the future, lock the balcony because the only people who sat there were sinners who left early and never contributed during the collection. With my young family in the balcony's front row, heads in the congregation down below turned to see which sinners were up there that day. The pastor was right about one thing, at least. I gave nothing in the collection that day. I took my money home.

This incident gave me the perfect "single incident" around

Ed Wojcicki

which I could build a case of frustration about the church, if I so desired. The next time somebody at church did something I did not approve of, I could say it was all part of a trend of insensitivity, because there was a time I was sitting in the balcony, and the pastor . . . and my story would be repeated again and again. How interesting that research indicates that the effectiveness of a Catholic parish is directly linked to the quality of the pastor's leadership.[2] But I have found this to be true in most organizations and structures involving large groups of people. The morale of an office is significantly dependent on the boss's leadership style. The service in restaurants varies so greatly in part because of the training and leadership provided by restaurant managers. The response of suppliers to businesses, when it is indeed good, often can be attributed to the insistence by the boss that customers truly be given top priority.

While effective leaders learn to soothe or cut down on the sources of frustration, no leader can eliminate frustration entirely, because not all frustration has external causes. Some of it is the result of our own perceptions of what ought to be. Some of it is the result of our failures and inadequacies and, as I have explained before, a series of disappointments. Some of it is the result of our discoveries about life, minor and major. At various stages of life, most of us discover we are not going to become wealthy, rise to the top of our industry, or get into the college of our choice, and occasionally such discoveries lead to crises in which our responses change the course of our lives. "Certain life crises, either managed or accidental, are inevitable," Gail Sheehy says in *Pathfinders*. "And all major life changes are potentially

74

A CRISIS OF HOPE

stressful. Beginning with the eruption of birth, proceeding by well-documented stages through childhood, there is a pattern: stable periods alternate with the passages in between, all through adulthood."[3]

One particularly well-known stage of life marked by substantial frustration is the midlife crisis. "Sometime in the ten years after they reach thirty-five, both men and women confront an often harrowing passage when mortality first becomes real and time suddenly begins to press in," Sheehy says. "As we examine the gaps between our youthful illusions and where we actually are, we may experience the same confusion and fears we thought we had left far behind in adolescence. Such inner turmoil has become well-known as the midlife crisis and is often concentrated between the ages of thirty-eight and forty-three. My studies indicated that for women the turmoil may begin as early as thirty-five."[4]

So to live at some level of frustration for a period of time is not all that unusual—not only at midlife, but also at other stages of adult life. Things go wrong, we feel helpless, and we get frustrated. The good news is that whenever we feel frustrated, we do choose our response. We can wallow in our frustration, we can fuel the frustration so that it deteriorates into bitterness or despair, or we can make a conscious decision to take decisive action to change our circumstances.

When we choose not to settle for being frustrated, we choose hope. When we choose to deal with our frustration with positive, concrete, decisive steps, we choose hope. When we choose to learn patience in order to work through the frustration, we choose hope. For hope always teaches us that

75

something more meaningful is possible, even when our circumstances cause us to feel so rotten.

Lou Jacquet, formerly the editor of the national Catholic newspaper *Our Sunday Visitor,* was surprised, to say the least, when he was fired in 1988 after writing a column that his superiors believed contained an anti-church spirit. It was a column about televised Masses, and most reasonable people would agree with Jacquet that the piece was not inflammatory. Nonetheless, he was out.

He could have lashed out with great anger and bitterness and tried to make of himself a national cause—the cause of a censored editor who got bounced for being honest in his observations. But he didn't. Despite the shock and frustration involved in being let go, Jacquet wrote a diplomatic farewell column that gave his 200,000-plus readers a Christian example of an appropriate response to frustration:

> [W]hat has happened has happened, and there are two ways to go from here: sink into bitterness at the loss of a job I dearly loved, or get on with my life. I have never found bitterness to be very productive. . . .
>
> I might think that old phrase about "when the Lord closes a door he opens a window," was a mere cliche had I not seen the outpouring of letters and prayers from friends around the U.S., as well as offers of help from folks I did not even know. That affirmation from the folks in the pews that my Catholicity is anything but suspect has meant a great deal to me. Nobody knows you better than the people who read you week after week, year after year. Painful as they are, these unfortunate events of the past

three months will not extinguish my vocal support for the church.[5]

What a diplomatic, appropriate and healthy response he had to the trauma of being fired! (By 1990, Lou was back in the Catholic Press, as manager of *The Dialog,* in Wilmington, Delaware.)

Still another example of a person dealing positively with frustration comes from Kitty Scanlan, the occupational therapist quoted at length at the beginning of this chapter.

After dealing with many doubts and frustrations, and even quitting for a time to work as a waitress in a restaurant, she eventually returned to the medical center, but with a different attitude. She no longer shied away from the circumstances that caused her so much frustration. She told her superiors that rules about OTs wearing white uniforms or lab coats and not wearing earrings were ridiculous, and won to the point where the whole staff no longer wore uniforms. Here's what she said after taking action herself to alter the situation:

Now I find it [being an OT] exciting, more important than the other matters. I see it as the kind of thing missing in a lot of people's lives. It wasn't the people higher up who didn't recognize the importance of our work. It was *I* who didn't recognize it. . . .

Through working on this job I'm coming to learn that I do have some influence, at least over my own happiness. I could have been here, wearing uniforms, fighting, being angry—feeling ridiculous, but helpless. Now I say, ''The hell with the uniform.'' And I do wear pierced earrings and they can't pull them off. I was lucky or smart

Ed Wojcicki

when I challenged them. They gave in, and now I'm learning something of my own power.[6]

NOTES TO CHAPTER FIVE: FRUSTRATION

1. Studs Terkel, *Working,* (New York: Pantheon Books, 1974), 494-495.

2. Bishop Victor Balke, Roman Catholic bishop of the Diocese of Crookston, Minn., in a speech given at the Holiday Inn-East in Springfield, Illinois, on March 3, 1989, in a speech about the importance of a collaborative style of leadership.

3. Gail Sheehy, *Pathfinders,* (New York: William Morrow and Company, Inc., 1981), 76.

4. *Ibid., Pathfinders,* 50.

5. Lou Jacquet, "An unexpected farewell to readers and colleagues," *Our Sunday Visitor* (Oct. 23, 1988).

6. Terkel, *Working,* 496-497.

CHAPTER SIX

Bitterness

BITTERNESS is ugly. It is frustrated anger. It is angry frustration.

Bitterness, unlike anger or fear, ultimately is a chosen response.

Bitterness goes beyond frustration. Being bitter is far more than being restless or discontented. It is much different from being depressed or despondent. I remember once telling a friend, after working through feelings of outrage about some circumstances involving my job, that I believed there was no more anger or frustration—just a dab of lingering bitterness. "That's a form of anger, too," she told me matter of factly, and I knew she was right.

Bitterness can happen to us. That is, we can become bitter without being aware of it or consciously choosing to feel so miserable. To remain this way, however, is our choice. It is an ugly, painful, lonely and isolating choice.

In the first phase of bitterness, the phase when bitterness happens to us, we discover we are not only angry and frustrated, but we also feel victimized by a person or situation and we think we have a keen sense of where the blame lies. Believing we are right, whether or not we really are, we may even concoct some plans for revenge and put ourselves in a position to be a wounded wounder. In our private thoughts we relish imagining ourselves saying to the source of our pain: I will get you, and certainly I will never forgive you.

The main character in Sherwood Anderson's short story, "I Want to Know Why," is an unnamed teenager who first became outraged and then disillusioned by personally catching an adult role model enjoying his baser instincts in a brothel. The discovery immediately resulted in outrage: "All of a sudden, I began to hate that man," the teenager said. "I wanted to scream and rush in the room and kill him. I never had such a feeling before. I was so mad clean through that I cried and my fists were doubled up so my fingernails cut my hands." Months later came the disillusionment and bitterness: "I can't make it out. Darn him, what did he do that for? I keep thinking about it . . . Sometimes I'm so mad about it I want to fight someone. It gives me the fantods [i.e., gets me very upset]. What did he do it for? I want to know why."[1]

Bitterness, left unattended, endures. It can become part of one's personality for an extended period of time, and gnaw and gnaw and gnaw away at a person's interior life. Henri Nouwen, formerly a university professor and now a priest in residence in a community of mentally retarded people in Toronto, talks about this in his book *Reaching Out:*

> Don't we often look at the many events of our lives as big or small interruptions, interrupting many of our plans, projects and life schemes? Don't we feel an inner protest when a student interrupts our reading, bad weather our summer, illness our well-scheduled plans, the death of a dear friend our peaceful state of mind, a cruel war our ideas

about the goodness of man, and the many harsh realities of life our good dreams about it? And doesn't this unending row of interruptions build in our hearts feelings of anger, frustration and even revenge, so much so that at times we see the real possibility that growing old can become synonymous with growing bitter?[2]

Nouwen explores with great sensitivity in several of his books how bitterness enters when life choices go bad, careers fail to produce spectacular successes, or participation in great social causes does not immediately achieve great changes in the world. So many people enter a position of leadership or start a new project expecting to establish a new way of doing things. They also expect to do a better job of attracting new members or getting more people involved in an organization. Such a raising of expectations is one of the exciting elements of starting something anew. Two days or two months or sometimes as long as a few years into the position or project, however, the complexity of reality becomes more evident.

As Nouwen puts it, "Many ministers, priests and Christian laymen have become disillusioned, bitter and even hostile when years of hard work bear no fruit, when little change is accomplished. Building a vocation on the expectations of concrete results, however conceived, is like building a house of sand instead of solid rock, and even takes away the ability to accept successes as free gifts."[3]

A friend of mine once expressed similar sentiments in wise street language after joining me as a fellow reporter at a newspaper. He had just left a job at a major national television network in order to enjoy the more stable life of a small city. Not too many months after he started, I asked him if the occasional bizarre actions of our editors frustrated him. He chuckled and then he laughed. "No," he said. "I expected something like this. I know that during the interview and on my first day or so on the job, everybody would say what a good place this is to work. Then I figured that after a couple of weeks I would begin to learn that things were not so rosy after all. They'll butcher my stories in editing; they'll try to stop our overtime, or something else would happen. It's pretty much the same way everywhere. Things never end up as rosy as they say in an interview, and that's just the way life is."

He kept his sense of humor about the situation. How right he was! Without realistic expectations, we begin to allow our frustration and then our bitterness to become the primary foundation of our attitudes. This is true in social organizations, volunteer groups, small companies, big corporations—in short, wherever people interact. The dangerous element of bitterness always waits in the wings.

Bitterness is so dangerous because once it arrives, it can settle in and cause emotional turmoil for a long time, even permanently. If it lasts long enough, its original cause may be forgotten but the bitterness remains, in people and in groups. What were the real causes, for example, of some of the bitter rivalries and prejudices that thrive in today's society? Does anybody remember? Why are bloody international conflicts handed down from one generation to the next? Why, in many communities, do so many high school students learn quickly to have a genuine disdain for the programs and students in the rival school? Why, in so many places of employment, do workers become bitter about management and managers express little but indifference about such bitterness? Admittedly, the causes are more complex than saying that lingering bitterness was not dealt with. But the fact is, bitterness is contagious and only gets worse if left unattended.

The second phase of bitterness is not when it happens to us, but when we freely choose it. Bitterness becomes a choice moments after we recognize it for what it is—an ugly, angry reaction that we steadfastly refuse to change or work on. I am not referring necessarily to angers and frustrations that we have recognized and tried to work through without much success. Nor am I referring to feelings that people suppress or repress while growing up, especially in dysfunctional or alcoholic families. Studies are beginning to show that in alcoholic families, for example, children actually train themselves to deny their feelings in order to survive, and this has crippling emotional repercussions if they never learn to deal with them.[4]

In no way do I want to suggest there are simplistic or easy solutions to discovering or dealing with the complex causes and effects of such deep-seated, painful feelings. For some of these problems people are well-advised to seek appropriate professional help and support groups such as Adult Children of Alcoholics.

When we finally get in touch with our bitterness, however, and we can name it as such, it should become clear that our own feelings are then a part of the problem as much as the circumstances we so detest. Author Charles R. Swindoll, in *Growing Strong in the Seasons of Life*, tells the story of his landlord who had been tortured and injured as a prisoner of war during World War II:

> Here was a man who had been horribly wronged—without question. The constant misery and pain he lived with could not be measured. My heart went out to him. But there was another factor which made his existence even more lamentable. Our landlord became a bitter man. Even though at that time he was thirteen years removed from the war, even though he had been safely released from the concentration camp and was now able to carry on physically, even though he and his wife owned a lovely dwelling and had a comfortable income, the crippled man was bound by the grip of bitterness. He was still fighting a battle that should have ended years before. In a very real sense, he was still in prison. His bitterness manifested itself in intense prejudice, an acrid tongue, and an everyone's-out-to-get-me attitude.[5]

Some people are capable of isolating their bitterness into one segment of their lives, as if slicing off a piece of "bitterness" about church, family or employer and living otherwise as emotionally healthy and happy people. While it is possible to be bitter about only one aspect of life, it is impossible to completely prevent this bitterness from affecting one's overall approach to life.

Not that I am proud of it, but I still carry feelings of bitterness about a previous employer. When I reflect on those circumstances and the years go on, I am able to understand cognitively that in all likelihood I was merely experiencing the real world with its pleasant ups and dismal downs. I can see it, I can explain it, and I can tell myself about it. But I still have not allowed myself to let go of some powerful feelings of bitterness, perhaps because in a weird and unhealthy way, I still find consolation in being bitter. It's called feeling sorry for myself.

Another area of life in which bitterness and emptiness hang around for years is in families. Legendary are the stories of unforgiveness in families. Many nuclear and extended families seem to have at least one person who is formally ostracized or ridiculed by everybody else, or if the ostracisms is not so pronounced, there is still that one aunt or uncle or cousin or sister who no longer socializes with the rest of the family. Often these rifts are never healed and everybody resolves the situation by saying that's just the way life is. Bitterness, then, can breed indifference, and in such circumstances an appearance on the surface that everything is under control may be an unhealthy disguise for hopelessness in relationships. For the family members involved, there is a conscious decision to live with it rather than deal with it.

Also in families, it goes without saying that divorces inflict deep wounds in people—not only in the couple that splits up, but also in their children, the in-laws and friends who have to establish new kinds of relationships and often choose one partner over the other. Feelings and attitudes of "what might have been" are common. Piercing feelings of loss and grief are also common after divorces, and bitterness is to a certain degree understandable. How sad it is to see some

Ed Wojcicki

people, however, many years after a divorce is consummated, still fighting their own bitterness about what happened, and still blaming others for the way their life has ended up.

In churches, too, many people—and if various studies are accurate, many *former* church members—carry on relentlessly about one incident or one priest or minister who treated them badly somewhere in the past. It becomes a bitter story when, years later, people are still blaming the minister for their lack of belief in God or their lack of hope in the church. It can be equally bitter on the other side, with ministers and church leaders falling short of their own high expectations and bitterly blaming a person or group of people—the ignorant, nonresponding masses, maybe—for the current chaos or malaise. Somewhere, somebody evidently forgot the great commandment to forgive one another at least "seventy times seven" times.

One's satisfaction in life has a lot to do with how a person responds to adverse circumstances. Gail Sheehy says people with low satisfaction "often become obsessed or depressed about roads not taken in the past. . . . Unable to make satisfactory compromises with their weaknesses or desires or to dare to take other avenues, they may become soured, believing that life is unfair to them, that they have been singled out for injustice, or that they are simply no good . . . They often become relentlessly negative and mired in the past. They look backward for scapegoats or flaws in themselves to blame for their current trap or dilemma."[6]

On the other hand, Sheehy says of high-satisfaction people: "The important thing is that roughly half of all high-satisfaction people have indeed failed 'at a major personal or professional endeavor.' What is different about them is their response: having failed, almost every one of them found it a useful experience and say they are better off for it.''[7]

Bitterness is a bad choice because it makes us live like victims instead of active creators of our own current lives. Since bitterness does not go away all by itself, dealing with it and confronting it are critical. Identifying bitterness and naming it are two important initial steps in overcoming it. Another important ingredient in the battle against bitterness, as the stories in this chapter make clear, is forgiveness and a willingness to be forgiven.

I will explain later how forgiveness is also an essential element of hope. If we choose hope, which reminds us that something more deeply satisfying or something more meaningful in life is possible, we reject bitterness as a way of life.

NOTES TO CHAPTER SIX: BITTERNESS

1. Sherwood Anderson, ''I Want to Know Why,'' *The North Anthology of Short Fiction* (New York: W. W. Norton & Company, Inc., 1981) 21-22.

2. Henri Nouwen, *Reaching Out* (Garden City, New York: Doubleday & Company, Inc., 1975), 36-37.

3. Henri Nouwen, *The Wounded Healer* (Garden City, New York: Image Books, a division of Doubleday & Company, Inc., 1972), 76-77.

4. See Herbert L. Gravitz and Julie D. Bowden, *Guide to Recovery: A Book for Adult Children of Alcoholics* (Holmes Beach, Florida: Learning Publications, Inc., 1985).

Ed Wojcicki

5. Charles R. Swindoll, *Growing Strong in the Seasons of Life* (Portland, Oregon: Multnomah Press, 1983), 166.

6. Gail Sheehy, *Pathfinders* (New York, William Morrow and Company, Inc., 1981), 13.

7. *Ibid.*, 14.

CHAPTER SEVEN

Apathy

PERSONAL APATHY

APATHY, by definition, is a form of hopelessness, and may be a personal response to bitterness or frustration. "What's the use?" becomes not a rallying cry, but a phrase of resignation, of dropping out, of giving in to indifference.

This can happen at many different points in our lives—in high school, early in marriage, after a few years of marriage or in midlife, in early or mid-career, or when the later years approach and finally arrive. There is an unsettling feeling of stagnation, of not going anywhere. Rather than mustering the energy to confront this feeling and overcome it, the apathetic response is to deceive oneself into thinking that what you have now is all that is possible—professionally, materially, intellectually, emotionally, intimately or spiritually.

When this happens, you can almost hear the thump of a person slumping into a chair and settling in for a long period of an unhappy, sloshing around existence. Gail Sheehy, in studying the stages of adult life, concludes people are healthier if they acquire a willingness to risk change rather than commit themselves to a predictable kind of continuity throughout their adult life. People pay great emotional and even career penalties by *not* taking risks once in a while. Says Sheehy in *Pathfinders:* "In my own studies, the people enjoying highest well-being were the most likely to describe having undergone a major change in their outlook, values, personal affiliations, or career. They had experienced one or more important transitions in their adult years and were justifiably pleased at having handled those transitions in an innovative way."[1]

Two-thirds of the unhappiest men Sheehy studied said they would like to change what they do, but they don't.[2] Sheehy also studied people who made the bold decision to change careers or start their own businesses later in life, around the age of fifty, and a time that Sheehy calls the Half-Century Reckoning. Such a "last-chance leap" does not have to involve an entirely new way of life. But it does require a significant change that will produce a temporary loss of security and perhaps a bit of depression upon losing whatever status was connected to the old job or old lifestyle. "There is a moment somewhere between the mid-forties and the late fifties for the person who finds himself coasting and unhappy when the last-chance leap must be risked if there is going to be a second orbit," Sheehy writes. "Beyond a certain point, too much momentum has been lost, one has coasted too long, and it is probably too late to pull up from the landing."[3]

This kind of apathy is closely related to experiences of despair or burnout, with which I will deal in later chapters. For now it is sufficient to summarize that settling for the bird in the hand over an extended period of time may be a sign of stagnation that makes it difficult to have hope.

A CRISIS OF HOPE

APATHY IN ORGANIZATIONS

While apathy in our own lives is an indication of hope-lessness, so, too, can apathy pervade an organization and be a warning sign that morale is low. But in general, I do not consider what is perceived as apathy in an organization to be as serious a problem as many people believe it is.

I have a feeling most of us first heard the word "apathy" in great earnestness when we were in high school. What student body, what student council has not at some point moaned about student apathy that is stifling school spirit? What can be done, the leaders wonder, to get more students excited about the school?

Interestingly enough, similar questions are asked not only in high school, but also in just about every organization in which I have been involved. At countless meetings I have heard people stand up to express a great concern about all of the members who failed to show up. "We need to reach out to these people," it is declared. Other common concerns are finding ways to get more volunteers and finding people who are willing to be officers. Although "elections" are required for president, vice president and secretary/treasurer for most voluntary organizations, the officers ordinarily are the ones who agree a bit reluctantly to run the show for a year. Once someone agrees to be president, everyone else is relieved.

And the $64,000 question in every organization is: Why do the same few people show up for everything and do most of the work? In adult organizations, this is merely an extension of the never-answered high school question about apathy. Although there are ways to build interest in an organization and spread out the work a bit more, my general response to these concerns is that apathy may not be the problem at all; what we are dealing with is human nature and the nature of organizations. Somewhere we should simply learn to accept that in most organizations a small percentage of people will do more than 90 percent of the work. There is a big difference in most organizations between the number of members and the much smaller pool of *active* members. It's just a fact of life, and it may get worse.

Consider what is happening in our culture. Just about everyone has multiple options for what to do with every block of time in his life. In many families, large blocks of time are now consumed by *employment* by both spouses in two-parent families, and, of course, by the growing number of single parents as well. At the same time, the number of voluntary organizations with worthy aspirations increases every year. So for many people, the number of options is growing but their available time to participate is becoming more scarce. This automatically means people will be more reluctant to join any bandwagon and will be more selective about what they will sink any time into. Their priorities will not be my priorities, and they will guard their precious time while protecting what is for most a very high priority—spending time with family members, especially children.

So what is perceived as apathy by the active members may simply be a growing trend on the part of everybody else to be more guarded than ever about signing up for anything. What is perceived as apathy may not be hopelessness at all, but merely a selection of priorities by individuals who choose to use their time for other purposes.

That is why, when it comes time to get some help on a project, general solicitations in bulk mailings or newsletters, while not a bad idea because of the publicity they achieve, should not be counted on to recruit very many volunteers or new members, except in those rare circumstances where an activity already has a tradition of calling workers in this way. The best way to get more people involved is to invite people personally and ask for their participation. Old-fashioned word of mouth and personal attention, while more work, will go a long way toward gaining the desired result.

This is not to suggest that apathy is *never* a problem in organizations. When it is, however, it is usually not *the* problem. Sometimes poor leadership is to blame (but the complainers don't blame too loudly because they don't want to volunteer to run the thing, either). Sometimes the mission of a group is unclear, or its current list of projects not at all stimulating. In such circumstances, the core group of remaining members and leaders is well-advised to re-evaluate the mission and purpose of the organization, and also talk to former active members to find out why they lost interest.

NOTES TO CHAPTER SEVEN: APATHY

1. Gail Sheehy, *Pathfinders* (New York: William Morrow and Company, Inc., 1981), 77.

2. *Ibid.*, 80.

3. *Ibid.*, 70, 232-233.

CHAPTER EIGHT

Burnout in the "Flee Generation"

THE race is on. The pace of life is hectic. Out of control, perhaps.

We are busy, busy, busy. Overwhelmed. By the busyness of our lives. By others. By our responsibilities. By our obligations.

Yes, we are racing. Racing fast. But toward what? Does anybody know? Maybe. Maybe not. No matter, no time to find out. Too busy checking the calendar. Got to run. To the next appointment. To the next activity. Got to keep worshiping that calendar.

The triple whammy of the dawn of the 1990s can be summed up rather simply: too many committees, too many meetings and too many organized activities. The era that was supposed to give us more leisure time has instead given us an overabundance of ways to fill up every "non-obligatory" minute. And people are burning out. They wish they could stop. They wish they could find more "quality time"— another popular term—with their children. They wish they had more time for strolls along flower-lined roads in the park. They wish they could change so they weren't so darned busy. But they can't. Or they won't. And they don't.

I have discovered in myself, as I have seen in many others, an unbalanced sense of overcommitment and overdedication. I used to say this with pride, as I would be asked with some

94

frequency to get involved in an organization, be chairman of an ad hoc committee conducting a special study, or join an advisory board or board of directors. The involvement of good people in worthy causes is essential, and we ought to sense a responsibility to contribute to the improvement of our society. But there is no end to the places where we could be of service, and there is no end to truly worthy causes.

I have also discovered in myself that it was not only a sense of dedication, but also a syrupy pride, that led to my over-commitment. It became unhealthy when I began telling myself smugly, "Of course they want me. They need me. They'll be a lot better off *with me,* so much so that I know I'm a much better choice than anyone else they could have selected." Such a feeling of being indispensable, whether at work or in an organization, should be an early warning every time that one's perspective is warped.

What complicates our seemingly uncontrollable *pace* of life is that we find it difficult to keep up with the many changes not only in technology, but in evolving social structures such as the rapid emergence of a significant number of single-parent families and families in which both spouses are employed. The changes have been unsettling. Alvin Toffler tried to prepare us for what was to come in his mind-stretching book, *The Third Wave,* which declares bluntly that human-ity now "faces the deepest social upheaval of all time." His definition of the Third Wave provides a foundation for why burnout is such a problem today:

> Until now the human race has undergone two great waves of change, each one largely obliterating earlier cultures

Ed Wojcicki

of civilizations and replacing them with ways of life inconceivable to those who came before. The First Wave of change—the agricultural revolution—took thousands of years to play itself out. The Second Wave—the rise of industrial civilization—took a mere three hundred years. Today history is even more accelerative, and it is likely that the Third Wave will sweep across history and complete itself in a few decades. We, who happen to share this planet at this explosive moment, will therefore feel the full impact of the Third Wave in our lifetimes.

Tearing our families apart, rocking our economy, paralyzing our political systems, shattering our values, the Third Wave affects everyone . . . It is a civilization with its own distinctive world outlook, its own ways of dealing with time, space, logic, and causality.[1]

The 1980s not only provided many telltale signs of the Third Wave, but the decade also witnessed the rise of numerous programs and books to help people deal with their new discovery of stress and burnout. Calling stress "public enemy Number One" in his book *Coping in the 80s,* Joel Wells explains, "Stress is the affliction of the twentieth century. Experts agree that on the conservative end of the scale stress is the principal or chief contributing cause of 70 percent of illnesses today—some say 90 percent."[2]

Stress is not the illness itself, but a frequent major contributor to emotional and physical distress. There is no such thing as a life without stress, and while stress can be a positive force and stimulate us to think more clearly, act more boldly and perform more powerfully, it is clear from the evidence that in all too many cases, stress gets the best of us. It overwhelms us, and burns us out.

The symptoms of burnout have been well-documented. "Loss of energy and the accompanying feelings of weariness are usually the first distress signals," psychoanalyst Herbert J. Freudenberger writes in *Burn-Out, The High Cost of Achievement.* "Pay special attention to tiredness. It's the best indicator for catching Burn-Out early, and although it's hard to face, it's easy to recognize. If you've been having trouble keeping up with your usual round of activities, don't fall into the trap of pushing yourself harder. And don't panic. You'll just make matters worse."[3]

Another symptom of burnout is a greater inclination to become angry. Still other symptoms on Freudenberger's list are detachment from people and events, boredom, cynicism, impatience and heightened irritability, an unhealthy sense of feeling indispensable, a suspicion of not being appreciated, paranoia, a kind of depression that is specific and connected to one area of life as opposed to life in general, a diminishing concentration span, and even psychosomatic complaints such as headaches, backaches and colds.[4] Freudenberger notes cautiously that any of these symptoms is not a sure sign of burnout, and that there are varying degrees of all of these feelings. But he does want to alert people that a denial that anything is wrong, even when these feelings are present, is "the real danger" in a burnout situation. He says in his book: "As soon as denial enters the picture, the person's symptoms become enemies instead of allies. They're no longer able to help, because no matter how loudly they cry out, no one is listening. Denial heralds a second stage of Burn-Out, just as exhaustion heralds the first.''

While those are the symptoms of burnout, it is probably safe to say the actual cause of burnout will vary greatly from person to person. Social psychologist Gilbert Brim, writing for *Psychology Today* magazine, provides a general explanation that is useful.[5] He says people ordinarily operate at a level that requires 80 percent of their capacity, so that there is always a little reserve of energy that is needed at intense or difficult times. When people taste a little success, they increase their level of difficulty so that they begin to need 90 or even 100 percent of their capacity all of the time. They begin to operate at breakneck speed, like trying to run 100-yard dashes all day long, day after day. They draw upon their reserve as long as it's there, and mistakenly believe the solution is to keep trying harder. The result, Brim says, is burnout and incompetence in high places. ''I've seen men who have changed careers when in fact they only needed three weeks off,'' he adds.

By leading a hectic, distressful life, we deceive ourselves into believing we are racing toward happiness and an undefinable kind of fulfillment at an undetermined time in the future. How ironic that in an era when new gadgets and other conveniences should be giving us more leisure time, we find ourselves drowned emotionally and damaged physically by the craziness of our schedules. How ironic that the very thing we believe we are heading for—fulfillment—is what we are actually escaping by the way we live.

If the 1970s produced the Me Generation, a self-centeredness that was bad enough, the 1980s gave us the Flee Generation, which is even worse. Flee Generation people are running so hard and so desperately and so blindly into the immediate future that they are running away from the two things that lead to real fulfillment: an understanding of themselves and intimacy with others.

The Flee Generation is burning out early, and this is dangerous for people in their 30s, 40s and 50s who should be reflecting on what they plan to do with the next twenty to fifty years of their lives.

The first step toward steering away from burnout, or swimming out of it, is probably the most difficult one of all. Psychologists often say that people heading toward burnout tend to be high achievers, and a person burning out feels caught in a gigantic whirlpool that is spinning faster, faster, faster. The first step is simply to recognize what's happening, not to deny what's happening, and to pause momentarily to reflect on the emotional and physical hazards of this downward swirl. Then capture that moment of peace, seize it, and preserve it, lest you get totally sucked in.

This is the moment when hope must enter, and remain. With hope there is always the possibility of change, and always the genuine possibility of something more fulfilling in life. "We humans are infuriatingly creative at finding ways to avoid risking change," Gail Sheehy writes in *Pathfinders*. "It is when all hope of change has been abandoned that one's spirit may break. For when we dare not hope for change, we lose even the desire for it. We submit to tedium, and our lives eventually become muffled."[6]   Once we take the first step of acknowledging the possibility of burning out, it's not an easy road back to a balanced life but at least we're heading in the right direction. A desire to steer away from the road to burnout should also make us strive to escape from the Flee Generation once and for all.

Since the three main characteristics of Flee Generation people are (a) filling up our schedules with busyness, (b) not having time for reflection and understanding ourselves, and (c) not having time for building intimate relationships with others; it's reasonable to say there are three things we need to do to become former members of the Flee Generation. One is to be less busy without growing lazy. The second is to find time to be alone for reflection, meditation or prayer. The third is to make it a priority to seize the hours that are required for establishing close relationships with others.

That is a tall, tall order, much easier said than done. Not even in our entire lifetimes will most of us learn how to do all of the things we really ought to do.

I have tried for years, for example, to discipline myself to have a time of regular prayer and reflection, all alone. It's so much easier just to say I don't have the time. I have tried morning Bible reading, evening prayer, Bible study groups, prayer groups, retreats, renewal weekends and daily Mass during Lent. All of them have been helpful, but all have been difficult to sustain over an extended period of time. I know I am not alone in this struggle because in every bookstore these days is an ample supply of material about prayer, relaxation and meditation.

What has worked best for me is a fifteen to thirty-minute time of prayer connected with Scripture reading and journaling several mornings a week. With some amusement I can report that my goal used to be to do this daily. That was an ideal but unrealistic goal, and one that merely set me up for failure. I can do it several days a week, but not every day. Not yet, anyway. I find that doing what I *can handle* is a big help to me in understanding myself and growing in relationship to God.

I have come to discover that understanding my interior life better makes me more eager and willing to share what I am with others. The more I understand myself, the more comfortable I am with myself, and the less I need to run around feeling half-crazy just to prove to everybody else how worthwhile I am.

But I have not escaped totally from the Flee Generation. Maybe a total escape is not possible and not even desirable, because the solution involves not abandoning what I believe in, but a better balance between an overloaded schedule of busyness and finding the time for quiet time and for building relationships. I still spend more time worshiping my calendar than I do creating time to develop friendships, and still have lapses in my morning quiet time. I remain all too often in the crazy race toward nowhere, and some days I feel hopelessly pulled along. Hard as I try, my schedule won't leave me alone—literally *alone,* quiet and restful, that's exactly what I mean—or rather, I refuse to allow it to leave me alone very often.

But as a person of hope, I at least am making progress at allocating more time for myself, God, and others. Freudenberger would probably consider my increasing sensitivity to the symptoms of burnout a great step forward. As he said in his book: "To succeed in averting a Burn-Out, it's imperative to continue monitoring yourself. Only *you* know when it's time for you to stop driving yourself. Only *you* can tell when your resources and abilities are depleted. You're the best judge of the gap between your wish to do [things] and the energy you have available for the doing. You owe it to yourself to keep tabs."[8]

NOTES TO CHAPTER EIGHT: BURNOUT

1. Alvin Toffler, *The Third Wave* (New York: Bantam Books, 1981, after the William Morrow & Co. edition was published in 1980), 10.

2. Joel Wells, *Coping in the 80s* (Chicago: Thomas More Press, 1986), 96.

3. Herbert J. Freudenberger with Geraldine Richelson, *Burn-Out: The High Cost of Achievement* (Garden City, New York: Anchor Press, Doubleday & Company, Inc., 1980), 62. The author's preference is to spell the word Burn-Out, but I prefer the more common spelling of burnout.

4. *Ibid.,* 62-67.

5. Gilbert Brim, "Losing and Winning," *Psychology Today* (Washington, D.C., Vol. 22, No. 9, September 1988), 48-52.

6. Gail Sheehy, *Pathfinders* (New York: William Morrow and Company, Inc., 1981), 77.

7. Freudenberger and Richelson, *Burn-Out,* 124.

8. *Ibid.,* 204-205.

CHAPTER NINE

Despair and Loneliness

Despair itself may be a desperate cry of hope

DESPAIR, different from burnout, is a tormenting feeling of helplessness, powerlessness and hopelessness. To be in despair is to be in pain, and it often means to feel alone, if not physically, then emotionally.

While loneliness and despair are not the same, I consider them in the same chapter because both produce a similar kind of agonizing, wrenching pain that is so tangible you'd like to rip it out and toss it away. If only you could. If only you knew exactly what to rip out.

First, with the help of a personal example, I will describe the difference between loneliness and despair. One time, during a job change that included moving to another city, I coped with the physical separation from friends by also excluding myself emotionally from the old circle of friends. I didn't write many letters, and on return visits to the small town that I had left, I rather quickly found myself reluctant to share very much about my new experiences, which were very exciting to me. Many of my former relationships evaporated—largely because of the coping mechanism I myself chose, and now regret—and there was nothing to replace them. It was a lonely feeling. In the new city I no longer saw anybody

Ed Wojcicki

I knew in stores or restaurants, the phone never rang, nobody shared my frame of reference and all I could talk about was where I was from and other superficial topics whenever I met somebody new.

On top of that, my wife and children were not able to move right away. Week after week of observing no progress in selling the house back home meant that the relationships closest to me—my family and my longtime circle of friends— were not around. Loneliness set in, despite the warm welcome I received from quite a few people in the new city.

I had taken for granted, before the move, how much energy and time I had expended in recent years developing close friendships. Even after my family finally moved and we settled into our new house, it took months for us to establish a lifestyle so that we could begin to extend ourselves again and plant new roots. It's so easy now to say "it took months," but living through those months, day after day after day, produced a grinding, agonizing kind of loneliness that only time could heal. So awkward did the loneliness become that we would joke about standing on the front porch of our new home and waving down cars so that we could invite strangers— any strangers at all—to become our friends.

Such is the nature of loneliness, a universal emotion that involves a longing for intimacy, an inner cry for deeper relationships with other people.

I had felt such loneliness long before the move. I had felt it even in the best of times. In crowds. In churches where the community is strong. At parties. On the job where working relationships were reasonably good. I knew in my heart that loneliness means not only being isolated or stranded,

104

but also feeling estranged from others, strangely alone or not totally bonded to others even when friends are around.

Loneliness is a critical issue for spiritual writer Henri Nouwen. He points out in *The Wounded Healer* how much time we spend trying to break the walls of isolation that separate us from others. Then he makes a point that not many others state so bluntly or so beautifully: We cannot get rid of our loneliness. We cannot escape it, and in fact, we should look upon it as a gift:

> The Christian way of life does not take away our loneliness; it protects and cherishes it as a precious gift . . . The awareness of loneliness might be a gift we must protect and guard, because our loneliness reveals to us an inner emptiness that can be destructive and misunderstood, but filled with promise for him [or her] who can tolerate its sweet pain. When we are impatient, when we want to give up our loneliness and try to overcome the separation and incompleteness we feel, too soon, we easily relate to our human world with devastating expectations. We ignore what we already know with a deep-seated, intuitive knowledge—that no love or friendship, no intimate embrace or tender kiss, no community, commune or collective, no man or woman, will ever be able to satisfy our desire to be released from our lonely condition.[1]

Discovering that we will never be totally free of loneliness should radically alter our perspective on just about everything. For starters, it shifts some aspects of life into a lower gear. No need to rush out today to force a friendship on anybody, because I accept where I am, and part of today's reality includes loneliness. No need to click on the radio or pick up a magazine at this minute when the rest of the family has gone shopping, because I can use the silence for a little while to check out my own feelings, one of which is loneliness. No need to fret right now about all of my incomplete irons in the fire, because my anxiety to fill every moment with "productive activity" is partially attributable to a fear of having to deal with my loneliness if I ever managed to slow down. How much different everything is once we begin to see that loneliness in moments of silence is worth exploring, not pulverizing. How much quieter the inner life becomes once we actually attempt to touch and feel and swim in our loneliness because of what it can teach us. The main thing loneliness teaches us is how deep is our yearning for close contact with something that is beyond ourselves, namely, close contact with others and close contact with God. How normal it is—as normal as loneliness!—to yearn for something beyond ourselves that will make us feel more fulfilled. How necessary it is to *have hope for something more fulfilling!* Loneliness teaches us to hope.

Despair is different—ironically, still related to hope, but much different from loneliness. It is more crushing to the spirit. It can be immobilizing, dominated by an awful feeling of helplessness and hopelessness, mixed with bits of impatience and antipathy toward other people or groups.

When I talk about despair, I should make it clear I do not mean depression, and in particular I am not attempting to define depression in a precise clinical sense that professional therapists would use. Despair is different from depression, just as it is different from loneliness. Despair is so common,

A CRISIS OF HOPE

yet identified so rarely as a major contemporary problem, that it is worth exploring how a person plummets into despair.

It ordinarily begins with a contempt of other individuals, psychoanalyst Erik Erikson suggests. That means, of course, something happens in a relationship or situation even before the contempt develops. Then, after another incident or two, the common route to despair involves expanding one's contempt beyond individuals to include entire institutions.[2] It happens more frequently than we realize. We see one government official using taxpayers' money to reward his friends with special contracts, and soon enough we project our contempt on all government officials and all of government itself. We see a family member mistreated by a church official, and soon we find a pattern, real or not, of mistreatment by all of organized religion. We cross paths with one corporate executive in our company who is conceited, arrogant and impossible to work for, and too soon we have contempt for all corporate management.

Emotionally, it doesn't happen that neatly and often not that quickly, but it happens. When I think of organizations about which I have had an attitude of despair—that is, a depletion of hope—often my rationalization includes not much more than one or two specific anecdotes. When I was in college, for example, I got involved in politics. From the inside, I became familiar with some candidates who I believed had little backbone and not much to offer. Then I was able to track the careers of these persons, some of whom were successful, and after a few years I was quite relieved that my own career did not lead me into politics. Since that's what happens in politics, I thought, I wanted no part of it. Sweeping had my condemnation of politics become, despite some good, dedicated men and women I also met along the way. What a despairing attitude I developed in a short period of time, and when I expressed this feeling to others, I always backed up my attitude with the same one or two foundational incidents. I saw that candidates could get elected by taking credit for projects that they in reality did not spearhead, and I saw that officials could get re-elected by holding back on what they really believe about many issues.

It is rather easy to understand how a general contempt for institutions or people around us can lead us on the unsuspecting path toward despair. The internal conversation goes like this, although perhaps not so clearly and not all at once: I see flaws in people of authority. I see flaws in people I once trusted. I see flaws in institutions I once blindly trusted. I don't like the flaws, but I see them. Does that mean I cannot trust them any longer? I don't know. Losing confidence in these things makes me wonder whether I fit in, or whether I want to participate in the mess. I don't know. Can I make a difference? I don't know. So what's the use? What's the use in trying to make anything better, including myself? That simple question, What's the use? can itself be a sign of despair.

We want to cry out in protest! But in despair we often refuse to do that, because we suspect that no one is interested, no one will listen, and no one will understand. We believe that all hopes have been crushed, and that all of our expectations of ourselves and others were hopelessly foolish. We tell ourselves the solution is simply to go along, to get along, to get by.

A CRISIS OF HOPE

The classic season of despair is the Christmas holiday season. This is the time of year when many are either reminded of past disappointments or encounter great residuals of family fighting. Many others, perhaps most of us, continually try to create a season of peace and bliss as we imagine it ought to be but never actually was, or could possibly be. For many people, December is a month when they drive themselves crazy with planning and activities and shopping and preparations, with the hectic schedule still at full throttle on Christmas Eve up until the instant when they have to go to church or arrive for that Christmas Eve function. In no month of the year do we worship our calendars and schedules more than we do in December.

Supposedly we do this because Christmas is a season of celebrating peace on earth and good will toward men. It is indeed just that in some ways, but in other ways it is little more than a symbol of how much out of whack our expectations in life are. News reports in the week before Christmas, without fail, warn us every year about increased chances for depression and disappointment during the holiday season. Carol Rubin and Jeff Rubin described for *Psychology Today* just how common it is for families to set themselves up for a Christmas crash. On Christmas morning, they say, after the presents are open, the scene is rarely like a Norman Rockwell painting. Something is wrong:

> The faces aren't smiling. Mom and dad, as well as the assorted assembled great-aunts and grandparents, all seem to have a sullen, slightly disappointed look. And now dad, moments after the presents have been opened, is proceeding

109

to scoop up the paper, trimmings and cardboard boxes, muttering something about "needing help with all this litter." The kids are fighting over the presents, nobody wants to share, everybody seems ready to gang up on some unlucky victim, and they all keep appealing to mom and dad to intervene. Mom and dad, of course, are puzzled, don't understand why this familiar scene is not a happier one, and are saddened that their efforts to create an idyllic family holiday have not worked out:

Holiday times are symbolic occasions in which memories of a fabled and glorious childhood help create expec- that are bound to be disappointing. Our advice: Be aware of this tendency and deliberately try to lower lofty expectations. Head off for that Christmas visit expecting to have a passable, but not wonderful, time. If you go off expecting something modest, even awful, then you will probably find yourself pleasantly surprised.[3]

While this seems like good advice for the Christmas holidays, it also should be useful for other holidays, such as the Fourth of July weekend family outing, and birthdays, which can also produce tension.

Unrealistically high expectations are probably responsible for much of the despair that has infiltrated our society. Somehow we develop high expectations of ourselves, our spouses, our friends, our children, our ministers, our government, and in our careers—too often forgetting how normal it is for people to make mistakes and how natural it is for people to go through phases of ups and downs in their adult lives. How interesting it is to listen to people who have been married 30 or 40 years. They usually say they are much more in love at that stage than when they got married, but they also say, often rather quickly, that there were periodic rough times. Probably there were even times of despair, when one or both spouses seriously doubted they could survive a crisis. That becomes relatively easy to say only in retrospect, and younger couples ought to listen to that and remind themselves during their "rough times" at two, seven or fifteen years of marriage that growing together means going through emotional battles together. If the expectations are that severe tension will never occur, couples will be much less prepared for it when it happens, and they may head downward from anger into frustration and despair.

Despair never goes away all by itself. I don't know where I read it first, but I believe that if we allow a problem or a negative emotion to go away by itself, then someday, somehow, it's going to come back by itself, too. A man named Goodman Brown, a fictional character in a famous Nathaniel Hawthorne short story called "Young Goodman Brown," had a bizarre dream in which he observed that neither his wife, Faith, nor a number of prominent townspeople in whom he had great respect could be trusted totally. Brown never recovered from this discovery of flaws in other people, and lived the rest of his days as a stern, sad, darkly meditative, distrustful and desperate man.[6] Although many people attended Goodman Brown's funeral at the end of the story, Hawthorne cast a final, bitter sentence on Brown's long life by saying "they carved no hopeful verse upon his tombstone, for his dying hour was gloom."

Ed Wojcicki

So despair can be permanent, and you might say it can be deadly, too.

Despair hangs on when we stop searching for a release of a sense of hopelessness and powerlessness over our lives. I see this in the Catholic Church in one very significant way, now that laypersons are assuming more and more leadership positions. They are told they will have a greater voice in what goes on, and indeed they do. The more involved they get and the more decisions they are permitted to affect, however, the greater are their expectations of what the church is actually capable of doing. As expectations rise, so do hopes— hopes for more active Christian communities, for example. While this is essentially a positive development, it has in many cases caused people to expect a kind of perfection that is impossible to achieve in our broken world.

On the one hand, for example, laypersons join a church council or participate in a cause such as feeding the poor with great expectations. But once they get involved, they discover that moving an entire congregation in a new direction is more difficult than it at first seemed. Every attempt to feed the poor produces for them a greater awareness of the magnitude of poverty in their community. After a while it dawns on them that their participation or their pet project is not going to be the cure-all, and disappointment begins to set in. So along with growing lay involvement nationwide is a growing amount of disappointment. In accord with Erikson's suggestion, the disappointment is often directed first at individuals (in many cases, priests) and then at the institution itself. For those unhappy with the slow rate of change, despair

112

has become an unwanted but real response, sometimes as people become victims of their own high expectations.

This does not mean that serious mistakes have not been made or that some priests and the institution itself are inculpable. Not at all, not at all. But that is not my point here. The fact is, no one knows how many ex-active Catholics are suffering from despair as a result of their disillusionment; no one can calculate exactly how many wounds of despair are still unbandaged on people who have simply dropped out. Andrew Greeley, in his 1985 "unauthorized report" on the American laity since Vatican II, comments at length particularly on the concerns of women and laments that nobody knows how many women have stopped going to church altogether because of bruises felt from the church.[5]

About two years after becoming a church employee, I came across a friend at a convention and began to unload my personal "discovery" that from a close, inside look, the church was far from perfect. I told about some people I knew who left church employment in bitterness, and many times those in authority did not, on the surface, seem to care. I told him I was rather shocked to discover that a powerful institution that stands for the highest of Christian principles sometimes uses that power to destroy people emotionally. "Oh," he replied compassionately, "you're entering your stage of disillusionment, and I hate to tell you this, but it's only going to get worse before it gets better." He was right.

The downward spiral of quietly despairing had begun, and I did not know how to stop it. Nor was I sure that I could stop it, or that I wanted to. I believed I might be a failure because I was not even smart enough to know how to cope with my desperation. As painful as that was, I at least took some comfort in Henri Nouwen's words which made me realize I was not the first person in the world to feel this way. He wrote in *With Open Hands:*

> Every time a despondent man undergoes the painful discovery that he has failed, he is ashamed and hangs his head. Finally, he becomes weary and exhausted from the tension of the effort to prove that he can do it alone. He loses the buoyancy of life and becomes bitter. He concludes that his fellowmen are his enemies and rivals who have outwitted him. This tension condemns him to a loneliness because every hand which reaches out for him is seen as a threat to his honor.[6]

As I plummeted into despair, I discovered that Nouwen was right. I trusted fewer people. I reached out to almost nobody, and was suspicious when someone reached out to me. I eventually had to teach myself—and this followed more than a year of basically wallowing in and out of various levels of despair—that no matter whether I was right or not about what I saw happening around me, I still had a responsibility to deal with my own despair. I still had to come to grips with the fact that I was losing the ability to hope for something better or something more meaningful in life.

Lest I be too one-sided, I must not end this discussion on despair without noting that laypersons are not the only ones who become angry, disillusioned and full of despair. So do priests. So do other ministers. Sometimes these leaders are more than eager to lead on the edge of change, but they find few real followers, or they find too little support from their own superiors or colleagues, or they find it to be a nearly impossible task to deal with many small factions each with its own narrow interests.

I have known priests anxious to lead their parishes into a post-Vatican II euphoria, only to be stymied by blocs or cliques who lament that Father is trying to change things too quickly. I have talked to many priests who work long hours but find it emotionally taxing to attempt to deal with all of the different interests that people in their parishes have, ranging from social causes to traditional devotions to theological debates about altar girls, and the Rite of Christian Initiation of Adults. No matter which direction a pastor heads these days on the ''political'' issues of the church, he will find supporters and adversaries, and he finds that many people will be critical if he doesn't move precisely according to their preferred model of church. A natural and sometimes understandable emotional response by priests is to have contempt for the nay-sayers and self-righteous people who don't give them enough flexibility to lead—and by now I have shown that a contempt for other people can become one step on the road to despair. So it is not uncommon to find that spiritual leaders suffer through periods of disillusionment and despair.

The paradox of despair, as it turns out, is that it is a possible response only in someone who knows what it means to have hope.

Only a sliver of hope, kindling somewhere deep within, allows a person to cry out in dismay, to plead for mercy, or turn to God in a prayer of desperation after not having prayed for years. These cries, these pleadings, these prayers are all acts of hope, painful as they are. Despair itself may be a desperate cry of hope.

I will pick up on these important themes and weave them into later chapters as they pertain to specific topics in this book.

NOTES TO CHAPTER NINE: DESPAIR AND LONELINESS

1. Henri Nouwen, *The Wounded Healer* (Garden City, New York: Image Books, 1972), 84.

2. See Matthew Linn, Dennis Linn and Sheila Fabricant, *Healing the Eight Stages of Life* (Mahwah, New Jersey: Paulist Press, 1988), 205-207, for a discussion on despair and integrity. They say in a footnote that despair can also begin with oneself if, for instance, people quickly blame themselves for feeling angry or hatred at an unjust condition.

3. Carol Rubin and Jeff Rubin, "'Tis the Season to be Fighting," in *Psychology Today* (Washington, D.C., Vol. 22, No. 12, December 1988), 36-39.

4. See Nathanial Hawthorne, "Young Goodman Brown," *The Norton Anthology of Short Fiction* (New York: W. W. Norton & Company, 1981), 589-599.

5. See Andrew Greeley, *American Catholics Since the Council: An Unauthorized Report,* (Chicago: Thomas More Press, 1985).

6. Henri Nouwen, *With Open Hands* (Notre Dame, Indiana: Ave Maria Press, 1972), 98.

CHAPTER TEN

Cynicism

IF A sculptor were to chisel a statue of the common middle-class man or woman in America on the verge of the year 2000, the final bronze figure might very well be a 20th century cynic—a person with a perfect sneer and a smug contempt for the most important institutions of these times.

It's in to be cynical, it seems—to be openly and publicly despairing about everything from government to businesses to churches. No institutions and few leaders are exempt. Smug faultfinders are everywhere; perfection is demanded of our major institutions, but the courtesy of giving these institutions the flexibility necessary to work toward perfection is rarely afforded. In presidential campaigns the national media have a supercilious field day with any perceived glitch in a candidate's performance.

In organized religion, even at the level of the local church, there is so much tension that evidently there is a handbook somewhere that teaches people to begin a meeting, after the obligatory opening prayer, by looking over the small gathering and proclaiming, "Let the bitching begin!" As popular as Monday morning quarterbacking in the church these days are pastor bashing, program bashing and lack-of-program bashing.

A longtime church employee once told me that one of two

things happens to anyone connected to the church for any length of time: Either one grows in faith or gets cynical.

"What happened to you?" I asked.

"I'm cynical," came the matter-of-fact reply.

Why is it so easy to come across cynicism these days, not only in the church, but just about everywhere? Cynicism can be an expression of despair, and when despair is nursed in this kind of release, it can lead to a long, long entrenchment in unhappiness. Do we really want cynics as our teachers and preachers? As our role models? As our news broadcasters who shape the public debate? Cynicism—a contempt for institutions and leaders that makes a mockery of hope—runs so deep in our culture that we have been deceived into believing that cynicism is an acceptable, mature response to the world around us. We don't have to look too far for well-known role models, either. Phil Donahue, the syndicated talk show host, was raised Catholic and went to Notre Dame, but left active participation in the church while in his 30s and is now frequently critical of the church. In his autobiography, in the process of explaining why he became disillusioned, he actually provides a textbook example of why people become cynical.

He describes "four phases" that he went through while in his late 20s and early 30s.[1] In Phase One, his consciousness was raised especially about the civil rights movement and the need to feed the poor. At the same time, his parish in Centerville, Ohio, was beginning a fund drive to build a million-dollar church. At first he joined the parish fund-raising team, but he dropped out within a few weeks. "Is

God more interested in stained-glass windows than in people?'' he asked himself. ''With Watts and Detroit and Newark burning, should the predominantly white suburb of Centerville be building a seven-figure building that, in an age of changing liturgy, might be obsolete in just a few years? . . . My answer in each case was no, and although I didn't know it then, my life, my faith, my attitude toward my country and my church, and my marriage would never be the same again.''[2]

Donahue's Phase Two was an angry phase in which he self-righteously believed nobody understood problems as clearly as he did. He got elected to his parish council, had his children bused to an inner-city Catholic school, became outraged by the ''lily white'' injustices he discovered in the church and American society, and he picketed the cathedral in Cincinnati. ''Phase Two-ers turn people off,'' Donahue admitted.

''Phase Three is a sudden, overwhelming realization of the awesome magnitude of the problem,'' Donahue wrote. ''It is a depressing awareness that all your meetings and all the rhetoric and all the excitement about 'making progress' is a self-delusion.'' It was at this stage he decided the church was unnecessarily destructive in trying to meet real human needs, and at the age of 34, he said, ''I had lost my faith.''[3]

That ushered him into Phase Four, where Donahue sounds exactly like my friend who said a person working for the church either gets cynical or grows in faith. ''Phase Four is where the saints are made,'' Donahue said. ''Phase Four people go one of two ways. Either they stay in there swinging despite the knowledge of their powerlessness, or they go the way of yoga, guitar lessons, astrology, psychiatry or plain unglamorous, uncamouflaged dropping out.''

Donahue became neither a saint nor a guitar player, but a national celebrity while moving his talk show from Dayton to Chicago to New York. Ten years after he dropped out of the church, he wrote of his own inner feelings, ''The big guilt is gone, the laughter is a little freer now, the anger has diminished, but the commitment is beige. I am not suffering, but I am not at peace, either.''[4]

Neither has he ever stopped criticizing various policies and practices of the church. In 1987, for example, after joining many celebrities and entertainers in listening to an address by Pope John Paul II in Los Angeles, I heard Donahue and his wife Marlo Thomas rail at great length about many church-related issues in which they opposed what the church was doing and teaching.

Donahue's four phases are remarkably similar to how some historians and anthropologists describe natural historical and social cycles. Anthropologist Anthony F. C. Wallace described in a 1956 essay the four stages of a major cultural change that I believe still hold validity. First of all, he said, is a period of individual stress in which institutions no longer provide the answers; following that is a time when people conclude that their institutions, and not they, are malfunctioning; third, the older generation will rise up with a reactionary movement and find scapegoats among the activists; and fourth, people's confidence finally begins to return, led by a prophet who serves as the catalyst.[5]

This supports the commonly held belief that groups as well

as individuals—indeed, entire civilizations!—go through periods of good times and bad times. They have ups and downs, joys and sorrows, growth and regression, normally and naturally.

Donahue acknowledged how emotionally unsettling the bad times can be and he described how a wounded idealism takes on a life of its own. People do not start out cynical, but first go through phases of observing, criticizing and becoming angry and frustrated. Only when these feelings are dealt with inadequately does a shattered idealism emerge in cynicism.

The fact that Donahue became outraged and disillusioned about the church when he was in his early 30s is not really all that surprising. Adult life consists of alternating stages of relative stability and uneasy times of transition and growth. Gail Sheehy, the award-winning journalist who has researched extensively the stages of adult development, pinpoints the late 20s and early 30s as ages when people are likely to question previously held beliefs. This can lead to a serious challenge of their youthful idealism. People in their mid-20s, by contrast, are in a relatively stable period, trying to establish themselves as unique individuals and doing what society expects of young adults. "Then comes the passage I have called Catch-30," Sheehy explains, "which usually occurs sometimes between 28 and 33, when the first sense of stagnation and discontent ordinarily sets in—pushing us to reappraise relationships, reassess our earlier decisions about career and family, and either reorder our commitments or intensify them."[6]

Since Donahue appropriately suggested that his Phase Four is where the saints are made, I wonder if it is equally appropriate to say that the early 30s is an age where many life-long cynics are made. Since this is the age when young adults discover in new ways how unfair the world can be, it must be a critical stage when they make choices about what their general outlook on life is going to be.

Keep in mind that not all cynicism is without foundation. People in authority sometimes do give those under their charge valid reasons for dipping into attitudes of anger, bitterness and cynicism. It happens all the time in the business world. For example, most employers believe they treat their employees fairly and with dignity, but objective outside studies indicate that the opposite may very well be true. Tom Peters and Robert Waterman Jr. call this "the lip service disaster" in their best-selling book, *In Search of Excellence.* "Almost every management we've been around says that people are important—vital, in fact," they write. "But having said that, they then don't pay much attention to their people. In fact, they probably don't even realize their omissions. 'People issues take up all my time,' is the typical rejoinder. What they often really mean is, 'This business would be so easy if it weren't for people.' "[7]

For the cynic, his or her cynicism often enters quietly, almost unnoticed and probably as a coping mechanism for dealing with anger and bitterness. But cynicism is not the opposite of hope, just as hate is not the opposite of love. Just as people who hate have strong feelings toward the person they disdain, cynics have strong feelings for the object of their cynicism, whether it be the government, the church or another person. When cynicism settles in, however, people begin to see everything through glasses crafted of absurdity and hopelessness. They tend to interpret everything in a way that merely confirms their cynicism. In a strange kind of paradox, cynics probably wish they were not so cynical, but their chosen pessimistic outlook leads them to believe that only a nihilistic attitude is appropriate and realistic. "Watch what people are cynical about, and one can often discover what they lack, and subconsciously, beneath their touchy condescension, deeply wish they had," Baptist clergyman Harry Emerson Fosdick once said.[8]

Left unattended, a wounded idealism that leads to cynicism causes emotional damage as it reverberates inside a person's heart. I am so fascinated by Donahue's candid admissions in his autobiography because, in a way, his story is my story. I have felt anger, been self-righteous, joined causes and been stopped in my tracks in my own Phase Three by witnessing the awesome magnitude of the structural problems in society, the government, the economy and the institutional church. I can understand why books like *Joshua,* the fictitious story of a modern-day wood-carving "Jesus" who is misunderstood and mistreated by church authorities after moving into a small town, has so much popularity.[9] Bash, bash. All over America, Christians are nodding at *Joshua* with approval because they have experienced for themselves sin and imperfections in religious organizations, and neither they nor the church know how to respond adequately.

The original Cynics of ancient Greece, a philosophical sect, were relatively small in number but important because of their eccentric contempt for the sciences and arts. The greatest damage done by today's diehard cynics is that they pulverize hope just when individuals and the world need it the most.

Ed Wojcicki

The problem for people of hope, or people hanging onto a
glimmer of hope while feeling frustrated or confused, is that
complainers are everywhere. To avoid them is impossible,
and once the griping commences, it becomes very tempting
to join in.

There is no quick cure for cynicism. The only one I know
is to make an attempt, when conversations begin to go down-
hill and all are once again on the verge of deepening their
commitment to cynicism, to be the stick that is driven between the spokes. Try to be the one person, or to say the
one thing, that adds an element of hope to the subject at hand.
One statement not only can stop a unhealthy conversation;
it can also become healthy food for ourselves that prevents
us from deteriorating attitudinally.

Like Donahue, I have not become a saint or a guitar player.
Unlike Donahue, I have not dropped out of the church.
I have seen its flaws, firsthand and up close, and cannot fix
the problems I see. But I take one cue from Isaiah: "They
who hope in the Lord will renew their strength, they will
soar as with eagles' wings; they will run and not grow weary,
walk and not grow faint" (Isaiah 40:39).

I take another cue from Donahue himself, who said the
saintly antidote to a sense of cynical hopelessness is to hang
in there despite the magnitude of the problem.

NOTES TO CHAPTER TEN: CYNICISM

1. See Phil Donahue & Co., *Donahue, My Own Story*
(New York: Simon and Schuster, 1979), 77-96, for a more

complete description of this tumultuous part of Donahue's life.

2. *Ibid.*, 78-79.

3. *Ibid.*, 92-94.

4. *Ibid.*, 96.

5. See Gail Sheehy, *Pathfinders* (New York: William Morrow and Company, Inc., 1981), 343-45, for Sheehy's explanation of the research of Anthony F. C. Wallace and others.

6. *Ibid.*, 50.

7. Thomas J. Peters and Robert H. Waterman, Jr., *In Search of Excellence* (New York: Harper & Row, Publishers, 1982), 239.

8. Harry Emerson Fosdick, as quoted in *The International Encyclopedia of Quotations* (Chicago: J. G. Ferguson Publishing Company, 1978), 190.

9. Joseph Girzone, *Joshua* (Altamont, NY: Richelieu Court, 1983; and in paperback, New York: Macmillan, 1987).

CHAPTER ELEVEN

Sarcasm

O NE of the ways in which cynicism, despair and bitterness are released is with sarcasm—with those bitter,
taunting, satirical gibes that are commonplace in conversations and a favorite tool of cynics.

At one time I did not consider sarcasm to be bad at all,
but simply a way of communicating or way of responding.
Sarcasm is deceiving because it can be terribly funny but,
at the same time, damaging to somebody else's reputation.
Sarcasm gets a point across, to be sure, but usually at the
expense of somebody else. How quickly sarcasm can sap the
energy out of a good idea.

Sarcasm builds walls. Sarcasm erects a personal defense
system more effective than walking away or not showing up,
because it allows a person to stay in a conversation without
allowing anyone else to get too close. Sarcasm is a major
obstacle to hope and intimacy—at least, it has been for people
like me who use sarcasm inappropriately.

I painfully recall an incident that occurred at a friend's wed-
ding reception. The occasion proved to be a happy time for
an impromptu reunion, as I visited with some friends I had
not seen in years. Somebody mentioned the name of a mutual
friend who was not there, and suddenly, three or four of us
were standing in a loose circle, exchanging denigrating stories
spiced with mean remarks about the missing friend. (Some
way to reflect on a friend, huh?) We did not intend to be

126

cruel, but in effect, that's exactly what we were, taking great delight in making sarcastic remarks about what this guy was up to. Also in our group was a priest who had been our teacher, and he had the good sense after a few minutes to turn and walk away from us. I realized at that moment—and it became even clearer when I reflected on it later—that this teacher's calculated departure was a way of teaching us that what we were doing was wrong. Our conversation disgusted him, and it should have.

I am still embarrassed about it, but still catch myself repeating similar behavior, years later, before I know what is happening. How often I myself set the tone early in conversations with a sarcastic gibe about somebody who isn't there. It's an attitude that says, "I'm okay and you're okay but nobody else is." Ha, ha, ha, but I fear the joke is on me, not on those who are too far away to catch my wit. So entrenched has my habit of sarcasm become that in the midst of opportunities to build relationships and new friendships—at those precise moments when there are opportunities for relationships to develop and the conversation level to go deeper—I defuse the bonding with the comfort of a quick sarcastic comment. The comment that evokes a chuckle can also produce a socially acceptable way of ending a conversation. Chuckle, ha, ha, it was nice meeting you. How sad that I often feel a mild sense of relief at that moment of separation. I had protected myself from the possibility of intimacy; I had protected myself from the possibility of having to give any more of myself to this other person; I had escaped. But the unfunny joke is indeed on me when the pattern of sarcasm and separation produces only a higher degree of loneliness, because I won't let anybody past my sarcasm and into my inner thoughts and confused heart. All I am left with are myself and my silly remarks. Sarcasm builds walls of separation, not paths to compassion and collaboration.

Consider what happens at many business seminars out of town. How often it occurs, especially at social hours, where one person tells a story about conditions back at the office, and somebody else picks up on it with a sarcastic comment and rather quickly the conversation is full of "Can you believe this really happens?" stories, followed by sarcastic gibes.

I often feel a pit in my stomach when such conversations end, even if they leave me laughing as I go, because I am well aware that we had just injured somebody else's dignity. For others, sarcasm may not be a habitual problem. But judging from the universality of "sarcasm groups" at social functions and in the workplace, I suspect it creates at least as many problems as it does minutes of laughter. Sarcasm raises suspicions about other people who are the objects of the barbs. With suspicions raised, trust diminishes. When trust dissipates, there is no foundation for hope.

So sarcasm can be a signal of hopelessness in disguise. The more conscious I am of my own sarcasm, the more aware I become of others' responses to my sarcastic gibes. I am grateful to the handful of people in my life who regularly challenge my ignorant, sarcastic statements. They either tell me about it, change the subject, or respond so seriously and intelligently that they effectively tell me that my sarcastic comment was not funny, but ignorant.

One day at a conference I was heading to dinner with some friends when another group of people we knew approached us on a downtown sidewalk. We had just left a restaurant where there were no more places to sit, and I cracked to someone in the oncoming group that perhaps he would really enjoy his dinner if he had to sit at the bar the whole time. I chuckled at my own "wit," but I learned later, much to my embarrassment, that the other twelve people who heard me either considered my remarks terribly inappropriate, or they thought I was a big jerk, or both.

I brushed it off initially, but a few days later someone else who was there dropped by to tell me how much my wisecrack about our mutual friend had disturbed him. The bottom line was that while no offense was intended, an insult was indeed the result and bad vibes interrupted a pleasant evening for those in my group *and* the other group.

I ended up sending a note of apology—which was all I could do after the fact—but I also ended up with another personal experience of just how far in the wrong direction a sarcastic comment can go.

CHAPTER TWELVE

Worry and Guilt

ALTHOUGH in important ways despair and cynicism linger at the bottom of the pit of hopelessness, they must not be the end of the discussion about obstacles to hope in the modern world.

Two forms of stress common to all normal people are guilt and worry, which can come to the forefront so powerfully that they block our ability to hope. Guilt and worry are cousins; they are related, in that neither is rooted in the present, yet each has the capability of immobilizing us and distracting us from what we need to do today. Guilt is one way of reacting to our past, and worry is an all-too-common approach to the future. As Dr. Wayne Dyer, a therapist, says in his book, *Your Erroneous Zones:*

> I worked with Harold, who was forty-seven years old, for several months. He was worried about being laid off and not being able to support his family. He was a compulsive worrier. He began losing weight, was unable to sleep and was getting sick frequently. In counseling, we talked about the futility of worry and how he could choose to be content. But Harold was a true worrier, and he felt that it was his responsibility to worry about possible impending disaster every day. Finally, after months of worry, he did receive his pink slip and was unemployed for the

130

first time in his life. Within three days, he had secured another position, one which paid more, and gave him a great deal more satisfaction. He had used his compulsiveness to find the new job. His search was rapid and relentless. And all of his worry had been useless.[1]

Worry is an obvious impediment to hope, a form of stress that often seems funny as we watch what others worry about. Much to the amusement of my wife, for example, I often have a mild anxiety attack a few minutes before we are supposed to leave to go somewhere. I get so preoccupied with getting out of the house that any little delay, such as a last-minute phone call or looking for a child's shoes, drives me into a panic that often finds its release in anger that is not exactly healthy but not very harmful, either. "It's time to go, it's time to go," I declare repeatedly, standing near the front door and hoping that everyone hears me and gathers immediately. Sometimes I'll go outside and wait just as impatiently, or sit in the car as if that's going to get everyone out more quickly. I worry I'll miss something, I guess.

Ironically, I miss out on more things than I should because once I arrive someplace, I worry that an activity will run overtime, making me late for something else. So on a typical day when I have several things to do in succession, I'll frequently fail to enjoy several of the events or chance meetings with people. I spend so much time quietly calculating how much time is left for that event, that the main thing I do is worry about what time it is. This inclination to worry makes me less effective because it prevents me from focusing on who I am with in the current activity. It is a kind of living

131

in the future that is neither productive nor healthy. As Dyer explains: "Your worry keeps you from living. A worrier sits around and thinks about things, while a doer must be up and about. Worry is a clever device to keep you inactive, and clearly it is easier, if less rewarding, to worry, than to be an active, involved person."[2]

Worry prevents us from having hope, of course, because, well, we simply cannot dream the dreams of a person of hope when we're too busy worrying about the future. Worry is not all humorous, either, because it can produce unpleasant physical symptoms such as backaches, cramps and ulcers. Some anxiety and apprehension are normal and healthy—providing us with creative juices in challenging times—but this is far different from the common kind of worry that prevents us from being creative or active or involved. If we spend enough time inactively fretting about a project failing, we very well might waste precious hours that could have been used tackling the task at hand.

Worry is a cousin of guilt. Just as worry can prevent us from hoping about the future, guilt can prevent us from having a balanced sense of our own past. Like worry, guilt can also freeze us emotionally, preventing us from growing.

One prominent social institution that breeds guilt is the family. Joel Wells, in his book *Coping in the 80s,* identifies tremendous feelings of guilt that many parents experience when they have raised imperfect children.[3] If this were not such a problem it would be funny, because nobody, of course, raises perfect children.

Feelings of parental guilt swell to higher levels among divorced people who hear all the time about problems of children of "broken homes." The flip side of this is that children in divorced families also feel guilty; it is well-documented that children often blame themselves for their parents' divorce—"If only I had been a better child. . . ."

Even among children whose parents did not divorce, feelings of guilt are mounting. Wells says: "Powerful feelings of self-accusation trouble an increasing number of American adult 'children' who believe that they have sinned against gratitude, affection, and responsibility when they send their aging parent(s) off to a nursing home or other institution which provides professional care for the elderly and infirm."[4]

The fact is, parents and children continue to have expectations of one another even after the children become adults, and in all too many cases, these expectations lead to hurt feelings and guilt. Children of divorce endure interior turmoil in deciding whether to spend Christmas with mother or father. If the divorce was particularly messy, children are sometimes made to feel guilty even for mentioning the "other parent" in the presence of mother or father. Newly married couples on major holidays often find themselves racing from house to house, from the parents of one to parents of the other, not only for a few hours of celebration but also to alleviate the guilty feelings they would have had if they did not satisfy the parents' expectation that they would show up that day.

Guilt that is the dominating motivating force in our lives is guilt that has become too powerful. In relationships such as marriages, guilt can be either a devastating motivator or a useful tool that helps us put balance in our lives. Both husband and wife in a marriage must negotiate a harmonizing act among a variety of interests: the marriage relationship itself, career (of both persons), having children, spending time with them, personal development and relaxation, outside interests, hobbies, friends, and extended families (of both). It is a lifetime challenge and constant adjustment of time for these various interests; tinkering with one affects all of the others. Some days I feel guilty for not spending enough time with my kids, for example, while other days I feel guilty for not squeezing a few more hours into civic affairs. Some days I feel guilty that my wife does not take enough "personal time" for her own leisurely enjoyment, while other days I try to make her feel guilty for showing up late from work when I had personal plans of my own. Guilt is both self-imposed and inflicted by other family members. In relationships, the balance is also affected by the *other person's expectations* of how *I* should be balancing *my* various interests. This is all right if feelings are expressed well, but keep in mind in most relationships the perfect balance is never quite found. Constant adjustments are needed, prodded occasionally by mild or major feelings of guilt. Guilt sometimes nudges us back in the direction of a more appropriate balance.

The big trouble with guilt is that the obvious solution—don't feel guilty when it is inappropriate or not necessary—is difficult to implement in our lives. The solution involves sorting out justifiable guilt from unjustifiable guilt, but I find that many people have trouble appreciating the difference and deciding what they should not feel guilty about. Part of the reason for this is that we learned guilt as children. We learned to feel guilty about disappointing people such as parents, teachers or coaches, probably without understanding when we were actually manipulated into feeling guilty.

A good starting point for adults, in sorting out guilty feelings, is to ask ourselves several questions: should I be feeling guilty about this? When I am feeling guilty, is my reaction reasonable? Am I merely giving in to guilt even though I should not be feeling guilty in the first place? What are my motives? Am I responding with genuine respect for all involved, or primarily out of selfish motives? Or am I doing it just to stop the other person from making me feel guilty? One of the great guilt-producing lines of all times—which is repeated often under many circumstances—is "I am only doing this for you." The unspoken knifing phrase that we absorb along with it is, "so you should feel guilty if you fail to accept what I am doing for you."

During my high school and college years my family, along with friends and cousins, would spend a few days each summer camping and water skiing together on Kentucky Lake. One year my parents were not able to go because my dad was nursing an injury to his foot. As the cars and campers were being packed, I announced that I was not going, either, with the expressed reason that I would stay home and spend some time with my parents. I somehow felt guilty that they had to stay, and somewhere underneath my expressed motive, I'm not sure I really wanted to make the trip that year. My older brother quickly pointed out to me that maybe my announcement about not going had little to do with my concerns for my parents but plenty to do with my own inner desires. "Are you really doing this for them or for yourself?'' he asked. I knew the answer immediately—for myself. My parents really did not want me to stay home out of concern for them; they could manage just fine. The guilt I was feeling was inappropriate and misplaced; so into the house I went, packed a small suitcase, and had a wonderful time on the lake.

It was a great lesson for me. I've asked myself that same question many times, in many circumstances, since then: Am I really doing this for others, or am I doing it for myself? Is my motivation based generously on a concern for others, or slyly only on what I want to do?

The first step in dealing with guilt always has to be reflecting on whether it is a reasonable response to something that has happened or something someone has just told us. Is guilt really appropriate? Should I really feel guilty about not going to my niece's baptism a thousand miles away? Should I really feel guilty, as a middle manager, that I cannot satisfy perfectly all of my employees' desires and all of my customers' needs? If not, the solution is to train ourselves—perhaps force ourselves—to make attitudinal or behavioral adjustments so that we are not acting weirdly in response to guilt. If a co-worker is disenchanted with his or her job, for example, and we have done all we can to improve the situation, it would be inappropriate to feel guilty, as if we did not do enough, if the person eventually decides to resign.

Inappropriate guilt is, admittedly, very difficult to squeeze out of our lives. We can attack it, attempt to ignore it, and make ourselves so busy that we fail to deal with it for a few hours. We talk about it and vow not to let it govern our decisions, especially big ones. So powerful and manipulative is guilt, however, that I imagine that even if I would ever reach the point of finally understanding the difference between justifiable guilt and unjustifiable guilt, and even if I would learn how to respond in healthy ways to all of my unjustifiable guilt, I would probably begin to feel guilty about not feeling so guilty.

In circumstances where guilt *is* justified—we know we need to spend more time doing chores at home or we know we have to watch less television and be with family members more—an early step in the healing process, along with making changes, is self-forgiveness. Guilt can propel us to behavior changes that are good for us, and it is all the more healthy if we also learn to forgive ourselves for something that is past and irretrievable. Forgiveness, in fact, is one of the most important characteristics of a person of hope, as I will describe in Chapter 14.

Hope means living as if we know something better or something more fulfilling is possible in the present and in the future. If we allow worry or inappropriate guilt to freeze us in our present patterns—by anticipating the future with anxiety or dwelling on misfortunes of the past—we prevent ourselves from becoming persons of hope. Worry frightens us, and guilt stops us from making decisions for ourselves. Both immobilize us and block us from the flow of creative energy that runs fluently in the person of hope.

The person of great anxiety, or the person who sulks in guilt, has a hard time appreciating how the present or future can be better. Chronic worriers and bearers of guilt are victims of hopelessness.

Ed Wojcicki

NOTES TO CHAPTER TWELVE: WORRY AND GUILT

1. Wayne W. Dyer, *Your Erroneous Zones* (New York: Funk & Wagnalls, 1976), 107-108.

2. *Ibid.*, 113.

3. Joel Wells, *Coping in the 80s* (Chicago: Thomas More Press, 1986), 23-28.

4. *Ibid.*, 28.

CHAPTER THIRTEEN

Bad Luck

FORMER Major League pitcher Joaquin Andujar, twice a 20-game winner for the St. Louis Cardinals in the 1980s, usually had the same explanation when something went wrong during a game: bad luck. How often he would shrug after a game, and rather than discuss strategy or the athletic finesse, he preferred to talk about bad luck or good luck. Sometimes, indeed, there was no logical reason that a broken-bat single produced the game-winning run, or that, on other occasions, a lightning-fast line drive with the bases loaded landed inches foul far down the right-field line. Nor could one predict when an umpire's split-second decision, later to be proved incorrect on instant replay, would unintentionally help a team go down to defeat. Chalk it up to bad luck.

I don't do it maliciously, but I often silently conjure up Andujar's intonation of "bad luck" when I hear a news story about a natural disaster or human catastrophe. When a bridge collapses suddenly and several unsuspecting cars leap into the water and cause the passengers to die, what explanation is there? I can accept with much regret that engineering mistakes will occur, but why were those people the unlucky ones who happened to go over the edge? When an emotionally disturbed person fires a gun repeatedly into a school yard or a McDonald's restaurant, what explanation can there be for dozens of innocent people getting injured or killed?

Every year we hear stories of death and great destruction, some caused by nature and some caused by human error. The year 1990 was no different. In September, three teachers were working side by side, preparing for the beginning of another school year the next day, when a series of tornadoes blasted through Plainfield and Joliet, Illinois. Two of these teachers in Plainfield High School survived; the other was killed, as were another twenty-six people in the area. Can there be any explanation for the storm abruptly ending one science teacher's life but causing no harm at all to the other two?

It was big news in the U.S. when these tornadoes struck, and equally big news a few months earlier, in May and June, when a series of rainstorms and flash floods devastated a portion of eastern Ohio near Shadyside. More than two dozen persons died.

Multiply that level of human destruction by 1,667 times, and you will begin to understand the impact of an earthquake that shook northern Iran in late June 1990. *Time* magazine used only two pages to explain that 45,000 Iranians died, another 130,000 were injured, and an estimated 400,000 were homeless. The earthquake registered 7.7 on the Richter scale. Had this been an American incident, it might have become the story of the century. Is there any reason other than geological that this quake crushed Iranians and not Americans?

During the time I was writing this book, one evening when I was relaxing in my living room, I caught a radio news story saying a college classmate of mine had died that day in a fiery car crash after speeding out of control on a rain-slickened Missouri highway. Carrie Francke, only thirty-four years old when she died, had been destined for success ever since I knew her in her undergraduate days at the University of Missouri. She was active in politics, and as a lawyer, was known to be a very hard worker. What reason could there be for her to die so young? U.S. Senator John Danforth of Missouri, giving the eulogy at Carrie's funeral, said she always held at least two jobs and didn't sleep much. "I wish I had been there that day [she died] to say to her, 'Carrie, slow down,' " Danforth said at the funeral. "She would have said, 'Oh yes, you're right.' Then she would have floored it."[1]

Why is Carrie dead?

Why did one of my wife's good friends die of cancer at the age of 32? Why, in 1976, did Congressman Jerry Litton of Missouri die in a plane crash as he was heading for a victory party after winning a tough primary battle for the Democratic nomination for U.S. senator?

It would be too flippant to call these stories the result of bad luck. Life-and-death matters are more serious than that. But why did a college acquaintance who probably should have been on that private plane with Congressman Litton not get on board that night? Why have I, on a couple of occasions, mindlessly driven through red lights at normally busy city intersections, only to be saved by a rare absence of cross traffic at those moments? Was it good luck? Alas, that's too flippant, too.

Ed Wojcicki

Some people say everything happens for a reason, that God sends suffering and injury to people more or less for their own good, and that God never sends people more suffering than they can handle. I'm not comfortable with any of these statements, because harmful afflictions seem to strike people randomly and without much reason.

Rabbi Harold S. Kushner wrote a book called *When Bad Things Happen to Good People* after his fourteen-year-old son, Aaron, died from progeria, a process of "rapid aging" in which a young person ends up looking like a very old person. A devout believer in God, Kushner argues that sometimes there really is no logical explanation for some of life's tragedies. He also disputes the often-heard statement that God never asks for more than a person can endure:

> I have seen people crack under the strain of unbearable tragedy. I have seen marriages break up after the death of a child, because parents blamed each other for not taking proper care or for carrying the defective gene, or simply because the memories they shared were unendurably painful. I have seen some people made noble and sensitive through suffering, but I have seen many more people grow cynical and bitter. I have seen people become jealous of those around them, unable to take part in the routines of normal living. I have seen cancers and automobile accidents take the life of one member of a family, and functionally end the lives of five others who could never again be the normal, cheerful people they were before disaster struck. If God is testing us, He must know by now that many of

us fail the test. If He is only giving us burdens we can bear, I have seen Him miscalculate far too often.[2]

What, then, can the explanation be for some people, most unfortunately, being in the worst possible square foot of earth at the moment disaster strikes? If "bad luck" doesn't cover it, perhaps it is not too far off just to say that life is not fair.

Young children in elementary school become experts at fairness, frequently to the point of having grave arguments about whether a candy bar was divided evenly or whether a brother and sister had precisely the same number of minutes sitting in the front seat of the car while on errands with their father. Whenever the scale tips favorably for another person, a youngster is certain to complain with perfect accuracy, "That's not fair!"

So parents and grandparents spend a considerable amount of time concerning themselves with doling out favors as equally as possible. Since this does not satisfy the kids anyway, maybe we should just spend more time taking the advice of my younger brother—that is, just glare calmly at the children, right in the eye and say, "That's right. Life is not fair." Not for any reason, and not because of sin, and not because God is sending in a new challenge or a wave of punishment. No, simply enough, life is not fair.

But in saying this, we must not abrogate a personal responsibility for our lives. We must not leave our future to fate, because despite the unreasonableness of some parts of life, we are not predestined to go down a certain track no matter what we do or what we decide. To say that someone is not totally to blame for his or her misfortune is one thing—and often very important to believe!—but to excuse people forever from dealing with their pain and ultimately having a mature response to their situation is different.

It is possible to learn from mistakes and to grow as a result of suffering. It is normal to go through a grieving process after a loss, especially the death of a friend or close family member, or after a divorce. It is possible to grow closer to God during a time of crisis. The processes of growth and grieving have been explained thoroughly and often by experts in recent years, and deserve the growing attention they are receiving.

These processes not only help those in pain or confusion, but they also provide many bits of wisdom for friends and family members who can help others work through their loss and pain.

Sister Jane Marie Lamb, O.S.F., in the 1970s founded a national program called SHARE, a support group which helps parents deal with the death of a baby, young child or unborn baby. The SHARE acronym stands for Source of Help in Airing and Resolving Experiences, and the Franciscan sister offers sound advice on what friends should and should not say when friends are grieving after the death of their child. Among the things not to say, she says, are:[3]

—"It is God's will." For how do we ever know for sure what is God's will?
—"It is a punishment."
—"You have an angel in heaven."

144

A CRISIS OF HOPE

—"I understand your pain; I had a broken leg once."
—"You can have other children because you are still young."
—"You are lucky you lost your child before you became too attached to it."

All of these statements, while well-intentioned, are often perceived by the hearer as insensitive. Sister Lamb suggests showing more compassion by saying things like "I am sorry," "I am sorry to hear about your loss," "This must be hard for you," or "I'm here and I want to listen."

Or, I might add, if you don't know what to say, just be there and be willing to listen attentively as your friend expresses painful feelings.

Although it is helpful for people to become acquainted with these healthy responses to loss, I am straying just a bit from my subject. I cannot do justice in one chapter to the wonderful research and thorough approaches to dealing with grief and loss that are already widely used. But neither could I wrap up this section of the book on potential obstacles to hope without discussing the kinds of life circumstances that often cause people to lose hope. When major or minor misfortunes strike—when "bad luck" enters, you might say—people naturally respond with anger or confusion, and may initially blame themselves, other people, or God. They feel victimized, and indeed they are.

Then, sometimes, they begin to live like victims, too, perhaps for a long time, perhaps for the rest of their lives. They lose hope in themselves and others. I have seen people who, although legitimately angry and frustrated by occurrences in their lives, never did find appropriate outlets for their anger. By not working through their feelings, they ultimately victimized themselves more than the original circumstances did. As Kushner explains:

> Getting angry at ourselves makes us depressed. Being angry at other people scares them away and makes it harder for them to help us. Being angry at God erects a barrier between us and all the sustaining, comforting resources of religion that there are to help us at such times. But being angry at the situation, recognizing it as something rotten, unfair, and totally undeserved, shouting about it, denouncing it, crying over it, permits us to discharge the anger which is a part of being hurt, without making it harder for us to be helped.[4]

Kushner also believes it is helpful to keep in mind that not only do I feel cheated and victimized and hurt and insecure and lonely from time to time; so does everybody else. Everybody is hurting about something. Everybody is at least a little bit afraid. Everybody is carrying some wounded baggage that remains hidden, because our cultural mandate most of the time is to pretend we have our act together. "[I]t would help if we remembered this: Anguish and heartbreak may not be distributed evenly around the world, but they are distributed very widely," Kushner says. "Everyone gets his share. If we knew the facts, we would very rarely find someone whose life was to be envied."[5]

A CRISIS OF HOPE

NOTES TO CHAPTER THIRTEEN: BAD LUCK

1. "Francke Is Eulogized As Pioneer," *St. Louis Post-Dispatch,* May 26, 1989, 4B.
2. Harold S. Kushner, *When Bad Things Happen to Good People,* (New York: Schocken Books, 1981), 26.
3. Rick Wade, "Things to say and not to say when a friend's child dies," *Catholic Times,* Springfield, Illinois, Oct. 12, 1986. Sister Jane Marie Lamb, O.S.F., belongs to the Hospital Sisters of the Third Order of St. Francis, whose motherhouse is also in Springfield.
4. Kushner, *When Bad Things Happen to Good People,* 108-109.
5. *Ibid.,* 112.

SECTION TWO

Reasons to Hope

"Hope that sees for itself is not hope.
For who hopes for what one sees?
But if we hope for what we do not see, we wait
with endurance."

—Romans 8:24-25

CHAPTER FOURTEEN

The Characteristics of the Person of Hope

MANY small occurrences and big events in the world and in our lives cause us to reflect on whether it makes sense to have any hope at all. Expressions of hopelessness in the form of despair, bitterness and cynicism greet us daily in world events and in the stirrings of our own hearts. The first section of this book considered many of these real and potential obstacles to hope.

Now it is time to demonstrate why hope is so necessary, beginning with the characteristics of the person of hope. Who is a person of hope? Fundamentally, the person of hope lives with the belief that something more meaningful in life is always possible, and that improvement is often possible.

A. A SENSE OF HISTORY

Perhaps it will be surprising that I introduce the person of hope with a short social studies lesson. But underlying all hope must be an appreciation of the fact that every new generation is the product of human history, and that every person has a personal biography with an historical setting that includes periods of triumph and failure, growth and regression, excitement and boredom. A person of hope has this *sense of history,* even if he or she does not have all *knowledge* of historical facts available in a university library.

Ed Wojcicki

A sense of history is necessary for the person of hope in order to avoid three common mistakes.

One is a tendency to think that a circumstance of the past ten or twenty years, or even the past six months, "is the way it has always been." With such short-sightedness, we fall into the trap of believing that whatever was decided last time must have been based on a longstanding tradition or must have been right, and we carry on regardless of the reasons the decision was made.

People born in the 1950s or later, for example, have little appreciation of the profound impact the railroads had on decisions that were made early in the twentieth century; yet we continue to base decisions today on solutions of yester-year—solutions that presumed railroads would always be the dominant mode of transportation. When I was editor of the small daily newspaper in Monmouth, Illinois—a rural community about 180 miles southwest of Chicago—I could not understand why our circulation was so good in some nearby villages but so poor in others. Then a local historian informed me that many decades ago, several trains went through Monmouth every day and traveled the same route to the same villages, too. The towns where we still had good circulation in the 1970s and 1980s were the towns where the trains fifty years earlier could deliver our papers every day, because they were on the common rail route. People became accustomed to buying our paper then because they could get the paper on the date of publication, and their descendants continued to buy our paper even though some of the economic and social links once provided by the trains were long gone.

A CRISIS OF HOPE

Another erroneous tendency of persons with no sense of history is to believe that some problems are being dealt with for the first time, when in fact they have been around for centuries. Christians disillusioned by imperfections in the world and church institutions, for example, seem to ignore the fact that biblical history and two thousand years of church history are bulging with stories about God's people messing things up as they struggle to follow his will. We have too little appreciation for the historical roots of much of what is significant in the church today, or for the struggles and creativity of the generations that immediately preceded our own. Even some Catholics who consider themselves progressive post-Vatican II enthusiasts often have little knowledge that "reform" and adaptation are always taking place at the grassroots levels—and that some Vatican II reforms had their foundation long before the council met in the early 1960s.

A third anti-historical tendency of people of every generation is to declare that they are living in the worst of times. This feeling regularly gives rise in Christian fundamentalist circles to the belief that the end of the world is at hand. In the late 1970s I heard this with some regularity from Bible preachers who warned us to do what we could "in the months we have left." No one can ever say with certainty that they are wrong, of course, because nobody knows. The first generation of Jesus' followers after the ascension believed they were living in the end times, too. "Never has moral decay been so rampant or occurred so quickly," we hear. And so on. But even a survey history course teaches us that some earlier eras have indeed been worse. Think no further back than Adolph Hitler of the mid-20th century, or the mentality of several civilizations that permitted slavery to flourish, or, in the church, about the bad popes of the Renaissance era.

Pope Benedict IX, for example, who became pope as a teenager in the year 1032, was one particularly infamous pope in an era when being pope was a corrupt family affair. Because of political plots and rivalries, Benedict had to flee several times during his papacy. To raise money for himself, Benedict sold the papacy to his godfather for 1,500 pounds of gold, and was eventually deposed. E. R. Chamberlin wrote in *The Bad Popes* that two years of Benedict's rule, while relatively peaceful, were nonetheless stained "with rape and murder, again commonplace, the remaining wealth of the papacy again squandered in brothel and banquet room and the upkeep of private armies."[1]

When crises in civilizations arise, so do possibilities for renewal. As I mentioned briefly in the chapter on cynicism, all civilizations that have come and gone have similar patterns of beginning, developing, flourishing, declining and disappearing. Historians Will and Ariel Durant, asked what determines whether a civilization will successfully overcome a new challenge, had an answer that I believe still holds a great deal of validity:

[T]he answer is that this depends upon the presence or absence of initiative and of creative individuals with clarity of mind and energy of will (which is almost a definition of genius), capable of effective responses to new situations (which is almost a definition of intelligence) . . . When the group or a civilization declines, it is through no mystic limitation of a corporate life, but through the failure of its political or intellectual leaders to meet the challenges of change . . .

To those of us who study history not merely as a warning reminder of man's follies and crimes, but also as an encouraging remembrance of generative souls, the past ceases to be a depressing chamber of horrors; it becomes a celestial city, a spacious country of the mind, wherein a thousand saints, statesmen, inventors, scientists, poets, artists, musicians, lovers, and philosophers still live and speak, teach and sing. The historian will not mourn because he can see no meaning in human existence except that which man puts into it; let it be our pride that we ourselves may put meaning into our lives, and sometimes a significance that transcends death.[2]

A sense of history gives context to our lives. We are heirs to all of the accomplishments and dreams—and failures and broken dreams—of our ancestors and of all others who came before us. This gives not only every generation, but also every person, a place in history. Such a sense of history makes it possible to have a perspective that is broader than the problems on the front page of today's paper. This broader perspective is one basis of our hope—a hope that teaches us that progress is possible, that noble responses to challenges are achievable, and that we personally can make a difference.

Just as civilizations have distinct stages of development and crisis, so do we have stages of development in our adult lives. With each stage come crises, some of which are predictable, perhaps not in their specifics, but certainly in the probability of a particular kind of crisis occurring within a certain range of years. I don't remember hearing anything about this while growing up or going through college, except for some occasional jokes about the midlife crisis.

Or maybe I did and failed to understand the message.

In *Pathfinders* Gale Sheehy identifies as many as nine of these stages of adult development:

—Ages 18-22: Pulling Up Roots, when we begin to leave the security of home.

—Ages 23-27: The Trying Twenties, when we are determined to prove ourselves unique.

—Ages 28-33: Catch-30, when we first reappraise earlier life decisions and first sense stagnation and discontent.

—Ages 35-45: Deadline Decade, when time begins to press in, we feel confusion and fear and experience the midlife crisis.

—Ages 46-55: The Comeback Decade, when perspectives on the balance between work and play "are all changing radically." For some this is a time of great excitement about life, but it also involves a danger zone with the realization that time is running out.

—The Freestyle Fifties, which is the happiest period of life for some people, especially those who do "not only the things one should, but also the things one likes to do."

—The Selective Sixties, when people truly sort out what is important in their lives, and ask, "How long do I want to live?"

—The Thoughtful Seventies, when people who are content, typically have made themselves independent, get involved in activities and still plan ahead for at least five years.

—The Proud-to-Be Eighties, when "the task is to resist a retreat into self-absorption," still plan ahead for life and be eager to learn something new.[3]

Erik H. Erikson, a leader in the fields of psychoanalysis and human development, sets up a similar but slightly different series of stages of development. In doing so, he establishes "psychosocial stages" and says that each aspect of psychological development builds on what is learned at earlier stages. How interesting that he identifies "hope" as the positive outcome of the *very earliest stage in life,* that of infancy, when babies struggle psychologically with the issue of basic trust vs. basic mistrust. How interesting, in Erikson's analysis, that it is necessary to learn at a deep psychological level what hope is before moving on adequately to other psychosocial stages where the crises involve critical topics such as will, purpose, competence, fidelity, love, care and wisdom.[4]

"Hope is, so to speak, pure future," Erikson says, "and where mistrust prevails early, anticipation, as we know, wanes both cognitively and emotionally. But where hope prevails," it eventually produces "a dim promise of regaining, forever, a paradise almost forfeited."[5]

So we are products of our times and always products of our own biographies to date. I find comfort simply in understanding that more likely than not, I will go through the kinds of crises and stages that Sheehy and Erikson describe.

Ed Wojcicki

I am not the first person to undergo periods of uncertainty and anxiety in adulthood. How often I find, as I tiptoe unknowingly into one of these stages and mention my feelings to a friend of a similar age, that the friend is beginning to experience the same thing. Understanding that these stages will come allows me to say to myself and my friends, "Do not be frightened by your feelings; rather, get in touch with them and do not let them consume you." Understanding these stages allows me to realize that as a mature and maturing adult, I will be challenged at times to take risks, because the alternative would be to stagnate and settle for mediocrity.

The person of hope understands that every day of life is a continuous part of a fluid history. Therefore, it is not essential to solve every complex problem today. It is not necessary in our personal lives to follow the business model of accomplishing something significant every thirteen weeks to satisfy the quarterly report. Nor is it necessary, or even desirable, that we be perfect adults, perfect parents, perfect businesspeople, perfect in relationships or perfectly happy in the very near future. A human life is by its very nature, unfinished.

B. HOPE AND WISHES — KNOWING THE DIFFERENCE

Besides having a sense of history, the person of hope understands the difference between having hope and having wishes and desires. Too many people, in planning for their lives and even in the way they pray, are frustrated by not understanding this crucial difference.

A CRISIS OF HOPE

Everyone has wishes and desires. Many people wish their income was about 25 percent higher, because they believe that much more money would make them quite comfortable. Many people desire a better standard of living, defined as more material gadgets, or perhaps one specific thing, like a new car, money for an elaborate vacation just once, or one particular job that they believe will fulfill them forever. Who among us has not desperately craved one particular thing as a birthday or Christmas present, and wanted it so much that our joy on the day depended on receiving that one item, no matter what else happened? This is not hope, but desire directed at a specific object or goal.

The person of hope is not free of such desires, but has a different general outlook on life because his or her happiness does not depend on acquiring any specific item or achieving any specific goal. I remember one year when the dream job for me finally opened up in another city, and I was in the mood to test my value in the marketplace. So I applied not only for the dream job, but also for another job in the same town in which I was living—fully believing that this secondary deal was a cinch for me in case the big dream fell through. What a humbling couple of months went by when, not only did I not get either job, but neither place even acknowledged my application! Four months or so after ''the dream job'' was filled by someone else, I did get a terse letter thanking me for my interest.

Had I staked my happiness on one of these two jobs, I would have been an immediate candidate for despair or cynicism. I felt disappointed and embarrassed, but as a person of hope, I knew that I would simply have to move in another direction. "Keeping your eye on the promised goal of health, happiness, and holiness is more important than trying to figure out every step along the way," John Powers says in *Mirror, Mirror on the Wall.* Hope, he adds, "does not measure how difficult the road will be, how painful the task, how much work will be demanded. It knows only that the promise of fulfillment will be realized by those with faith strong enough to keep on trying."[6]

This does not mean that goal-setting is a bad idea or that planning is a waste of time. Plans and goals give direction to our lives, and as Powers suggests, having an "imagined goal" can actually increase our hope in difficult times. There is also value in knowing about self-fulfilling prophecies, which teach us that believing we will fail can actually increase the likelihood that we will fail. And there is a similar problem in setting goals that are too low or too soft; these goals are not challenging enough. The real problem comes when we consider the goal synonymous with hope—when we begin to believe our happiness depends on the achievement of a single goal that is quite specific and inflexible.

We misplace our hope, for example, by saying we want our children to be the brightest students in their class; a much healthier "goal of hope" is to say we will assist our children in learning good study skills so they can be very good students. We misplace our hope by saying our business will be number one in the community or in the world; a much better approach is to set challenging goals for our business and to say we will learn as much as we can and focus on performing as efficiently as possible, even as we vigorously pursue the specific quarterly or annual goals.

C. PATIENCE AND ACCEPTANCE

I volunteered one of my college summers to be the press secretary for a candidate for Congress. Election night delivered the kind of excitement that a close race is supposed to bring. The campaign's leaders gathered privately with the candidate to watch the results on television, and after a few hours it became clear that we were going to lose by about 1,000 votes out of more than 80,000 cast. The candidate's wife broke the tension a bit by saying philosophically to her husband, "Oh well. Maybe God has something else in store for you."

The candidate, an experienced state legislator and a good, highly principled man, responded by slumping onto the couch with a sigh and saying, "Well, if he does, I wish he'd hurry up and tell me what it is." Just a few years earlier, this man had lost another close election, that time for a statewide office.

The person of hope is not, by any means, a person free of disappointment, doubts, or misfortune. On the contrary, as a person with a sense of history, the person of hope is actually prepared for unexpected turns in his or her plan. As a person who understands the difference between hope and desires, the person of hope has the flexibility to accept that there will be disappointing delays and crushing defeats, and that adjustments in dreams and plans will be necessary, sometimes very quickly.

Ed Wojcicki

As St. Paul wrote in the Romans about 56 A.D. "[W]e even boast of our afflictions, knowing that affliction produces endurance, and endurance, proven character, and proven character, hope . . ." (Romans 5:3-4).

This kind of acceptance does not imply an acceptance of lackluster efforts or a despairing resignation that mediocrity is all that is ever possible. But to have a healthy perspective on any situation, a necessary step is always to accept the objective facts for what they are, so that they can be addressed appropriately. That is why I spent so much time in the first section of the book looking at topics such as anger, frustration and cynicism. If we never learn to identify these internal feelings, we handicap our ability to deal with the tensions in our lives.

"Acceptance" requires patience, reflection and time. Particularly as people deal with loss or death, they go through a series of emotional stages, each of which requires time for processing and reckoning. Dr. Elisabeth Kubler-Ross describes these stages of grieving as denial, anger, bargaining, depression, and finally, acceptance, and explains in detail in her well-known work on death and dying the importance of each state.[7] Many others in the past two decades have applied these or similar stages to the process of healing emotional pain caused by incidents other than death, such as divorce.

Even when there is a basic acceptance of this process of emotional healing, another attribute specifically needed in most circumstances is patience, one of the most difficult virtues in a world that demands and reveres tangible, quick-and-easy results. Intellectually, it is so easy to say that the

162

complexity of many problems will take time to heal. But how difficult it is, in the daily grind, to have the patience to persevere and to let events develop smoothly in a gradual process. How unfortunate that we have been unwittingly conditioned by 30-minute television programs and 90-minute movies to believe that human conflicts can be resolved in short amounts of time. How appropriate that in St. Paul's famous description of love in the thirteenth chapter of First Corinthians, the very first thing he says is, "Love is patient. . . ."

It might seem difficult at first to understand how a person can learn patience and acceptance and at the same time, not settle for mediocrity. Keep in mind that the person of hope never loses the deeply held belief that something better or something more meaningful in life is possible. People of hope accept, however, that their own idea of how progress should occur may not in fact develop. Neither might their personal contribution to the change be significant, and neither might their secret, personal timetable for working things out prove to be accurate. With such humility, people of hope are well-equipped to confront new challenges. So people of hope do not at all mind exploring and living on the edge of change, or as John Powers says, "on the edge of failure."[8] Hope equips and prepares them simultaneously for progress or setbacks.

It is this kind of saintly hope, I am convinced, that allows people to battle for years against apartheid in South Africa, against abortion in the United States, or against significant obstacles to more harmonious relationships in their daily affairs, without burning out.

Ed Wojcicki

A woman I know has stayed in a job for many years despite the presence of a boss who, by all accounts, is difficult to work for. But her focus has been on the assistance given to others through their business. I am convinced hope has taught her that her work is more meaningful than the internal operations of the office, and that "her way"—even though better—is not as important as getting the help to those who need it.

I sometimes wonder, as I go about my own busy schedule and try to make a difference, whether all of my "work" will ultimately prove to be far less valuable than the time I put into being a parent. Maybe what I am called to be most of all, on top of my career and community involvement, is the best possible example for my children. Maybe not I but one of my children, or perhaps one of their children, is called to accomplish something strikingly significant for humankind. Or maybe none of us is. This helps me understand that hope has less to do with personal accomplishments than it does with believing that our lives have great meaning, and that something more meaningful is always possible. This kind of reflection gives me perspective, it teaches me patience, and it gives me hope.

D. A FORGIVING HEART

A willingness to forgive is a natural development for a person who learns patience and acceptance. Since hope involves a longing for something better or something more meaningful, and human failings so often get in the way of progress, forgiveness of those responsible for the obstacles is necessary.

Forgiveness makes it possible for us always to be prepared

164

to see the other person, the troubling situation, and ourselves, renewed. The act of forgiveness makes it possible to begin anew and to hope once again for something better. Without forgiveness, hope is impossible to sustain. Forgiveness is the switch that sheds a bright, new, hopeful light on our lives.

I remember once when giving a talk about living a Christian life, I referred to a person who had wounded me emotionally a year earlier. I declared in my talk that I was not ready to forgive that person. I felt justified in my anger, and cynicism became my crutch. I was stubborn, but I was also very hurt. Now that I look back on those circumstances, I can see how my stubbornness and refusal to forgive led me quickly down the path of anger and bitterness for more than a year. I also see now that it was during this time that I was about as close as I could be to not having any hope.

In *Healing Wounded Emotions,* Martin Padovani makes the important distinction between an *act* of forgiveness and a *feeling* of forgiveness.[9] The act is very important and may occur long before the feeling arrives. Forgiving does not mean immediately forgetting. Padovani writes:

> Even when we forgive, resentful feelings are often still present and this is all right; but if we act in a resentful way, it is sinful. . . . The truth is that we can genuinely forgive even though time is required to forget and to heal our negative feelings. We have to live with those feelings for a while. The divorced, the victims of crime, injustice, terrorism and war, parents hurt and rejected by their children, children neglected and mistreated by their parents, the old who are overlooked and the young who are not

165

heard—all who suffer the hurts, misunderstandings, and insensitivities of daily living can forgive, but we must realize that forgetting will take time.

Just as we must learn to forgive others and give our feelings time to be healed, we must also learn, when we harm others, to humbly give them an opportunity to forgive us, and to give them the time they need for their feelings to be healed regarding us.

Also not to be overlooked, is the importance of forgiving ourselves when we have wronged others. If we fail to forgive ourselves, we can become saddled with guilt and despair. If we lose hope in ourselves, we lose hope, period.

E. HOPE IN OURSELVES

There is a great temptation, in exploring the idea of hoping in ourselves, to restate all that has been written in recent decades about allocating enough time for working, playing and praying. There is so much valuable advice in books these days about maintaining our emotional health, having enough time (or any time at all) for relaxation, and improving our relationships with others. Much has also been written about the importance of self-esteem and the many reasons for low self-esteem in modern American society.

One point that can never get enough attention, because so few seem to know how to accomplish it, is the almost impossible idea of breaking from the kind of American lifestyle that keeps us so terribly busy all the time—the phenomenon I call the worship of our calendars. I talked about this in the chapter on burnout while discussing the desperation of "Flee Generation" people of the 1980s. One attribute of Flee Generation people is not allotting enough time simply to get to know ourselves and to explore our own inner thoughts and feelings. Henri Nouwen, for whom the concept of solitude is so crucial, describes modern-day scurrying perfectly in his book, *The Way of the Heart:*

> In general we are very busy people. We have many meetings to attend, many visits to make, many [worship] services to lead. Our calendars are filled with appointments, our days and weeks filled with engagements, and our years filled with plans and projects. There is seldom a period in which we do not know what to do, and we move through life in such a distracted way that we do not even take the time and rest to wonder if any of the things we think, say, or do are *worth* thinking, saying, or doing . . . Thus we are very busy people just like all other busy people, rewarded with the rewards which are rewarded to busy people![10]

Asking how much time we spend getting to know ourselves is different from asking whether we have any time for leisure activities or relaxation. I know that my own routine, from the time I wake up until I retire every night, is spent either at work, with my children, with my wife, with other people, working on projects or chores, filling whatever hours remain with a little television or listening to St. Louis Cardinals' baseball games on the radio. Some of this is time very well-spent, of course.

But if I want to be a person of hope, I should have the courtesy to also find enough time to get to know the very person—myself—whom I believe should be a witness of hope to the world. For if I do not really know this person, how can I know that it is necessary that *I* have hope? So I ask myself: How much time do I spend with no books, no radio, and no other people, with absolutely no distractions at all, so that I can get closely in touch with what is happening in the stirrings of my heart? The answer for myself, and for most others I know, is very, very little. Certainly not enough.

For Nouwen, solitude is not the same as slicing off enough privacy time to recharge our batteries and think interesting thoughts and prepare to re-enter the competitive world re-freshed. No, solitude becomes the place where, without phone calls or meetings or books, we actually confront ourselves, "just me—naked, vulnerable, weak, sinful, deprived, broken—nothing. It is this nothingness that I have to face in my solitude, a nothingness so dreadful that everything in me wants to run to my friends, my work, and my distrac-tions so that I can forget my nothingness and make myself believe that I am worth something."[11]

I know how quickly I flee from opportunities for solitude. When my children were still babies and it was my turn to stay home while my wife went shopping or out with friends, I would initially relish the opportunity to get a few things done at home. But not long after my wife would leave, I would catch myself pacing rather aimlessly around the house, or heading almost unconsciously for the telephone, perhaps to call a friend or other family member long distance just to chat. Just to chat? Of course not! What I was doing was beating down the fear of being alone with myself for too long.

I have since become more comfortable, early in the mornings or late at night especially, just sitting on the couch, sometimes with a Bible and my personal journal nearby, enjoying some private reflections on the occurrences of the day or the current causes of tension in my life. Being more comfortable being alone with myself makes it possible to have more hope in myself. I must be careful to say that hoping in myself is not the same as believing that I can do all things by myself, that I can do anything I attempt to do, or that I alone possess all of the resources I will ever need to be successful. These attitudes can lead to an idolatry of selfishness that ultimately produces self-righteousness or bitterness.

No, by being comfortable with myself and learning to love myself more despite my brokenness and secret feelings of insecurity and inferiority, I begin to see more clearly, within the context of my sense of history, that I can make a difference. I begin to hope more fully that something better really is possible, especially as I get more closely in touch with where I fit in and what contribution is truly possible for me. More importantly, in my solitude I begin to acquire the perspective that something more deeply satisfying in life is always possible—not in the sense of being nervously unsatisfied with what I have or where I am, but in the sense that my life has a meaning that has little to do with all of my immediate concerns.

I also begin to understand that hope is not hope unless I share it with others.

Ed Wojcicki

F. HOPE IN OTHERS

The final characteristic of the person of hope is having hope in others. It is knowing that I am not responsible by myself for bringing hope to a troubled world.

Sometimes we hear the opposite message. We hear that it is foolish to rely on others because they are certain to disappoint us. We tell ourselves, "If I don't do this, nobody else will," and indeed, sometimes that is true. We ask ourselves what is the use of asking others to help because few will respond.

The answer lies in the power of a community and the power of intimacy.

Once at a local Pax Christi meeting—an international Catholic social justice organization in which I am interested but not really active—I heard an explanation of community power I will never forget. The speaker reminded the small gathering how important it is that the group continue to meet to discuss disarmament, Central America and other topics. The Pax Christi numbers are small, and they are small in the next town and the one after that, too, she noted. But taken together, their numbers add up, and because of these numerous grassroots gatherings in one city after another, there is indeed a national voice that becomes a Christian peace movement. Such is power not only of the peace movement, but of every cause. A cause becomes a cause precisely because someone or a small group has hope for something better and is willing to risk seeking a few small links of support. Concrete examples of this today are numerous—students craving for

170

A CRISIS OF HOPE

democratic reform in China, Solidarity members seeking the same in Poland, Habitat for Humanity members building houses for the poor in the U.S., to name just three.

The person of hope seeks not only to collaborate with others, but also to be energized by pursuing intimacy, the kinds of close friendships in which feelings and aspirations are shared with another person openly, frequently and freely. This takes time, effort, patience, energy, and real sacrifices. That is why I have identified a flight from intimacy as the second noteworthy trademark of Flee Generation people, who avoid intimacy as much as they avoid getting to know themselves. With creative, sweet-sounding, face-saving language, we justify not taking time to build intimate friendships. We worship our calendars and deceive ourselves into believing that being busy is more important. We cannot sacrifice any of our projects because there is so much *we* have to do, and if intimacy falls by the wayside, well, that's what happens in modern America, we say.

But the person of hope moves naturally in the direction of intimacy, because hope teaches that something more meaningful and deeply satisfying beyond ourselves is possible. Exactly what is it beyond ourselves that is more meaningful? Our response to this hope is love, and in loving other people are fertile opportunities for intimacy. Love and intimacy are not identical, of course, because we can love many people but be intimate with only a few at a time. But as love is the object of our hope, hope certainly sets the stage for intimacy. Whenever we craftily impede the possibility of intimacy with others, we cut off what is a natural longing for bonding with other people. We cut off a slice of hope that helps us see that something more meaningful in life beyond ourselves is always out there. We cut off an enormously important source of strength and energy for ourselves as well. Therapist Clayton Barbeau, speaking at the national convention of the Christian Family Movement, said intimacy makes us feel more alive, more energized. If it's real love, he said, we feel energized—so energized that we want to go out and do more things and love even more people.[12] On the other hand, if it's only infatuation or lust, a person may not feel energized, but primarily trapped and drained by the relationship. So it is sadly ironic that by pursuing what we believe are worthy goals and fulfilling projects to the exclusion of intimate friendships, we are sacrificing one of the sources of energy that would simultaneously allow us to bring hope, vigorously and enthusiastically, to the world.

Joyce Landorf Heatherley describes this reality by saying all of us have "basement people" and "balcony people" in our lives. In her book *Balcony People,* she labels basement people those who pull us down, who tell us we cannot do such and such, and demoralize us with subtle or not so subtle expressions of their low expectations for us.[13] Balcony people, on the other hand, are up there in the balcony of our lives, applauding and giving us standing ovations and cheering us on. Quoting the kind of cheering a balcony person does, she says, "I believe in you. I'm leaning way, way over your balcony railing; I'm waving my coat above my head, and I'm yelling above the frightening noises of your world, 'I love you! I believe in you and your abilities! You can do it! Keep at it. Keep on!' "[14]

A CRISIS OF HOPE

Such an attitude of enthusiasm and affirmation clearly is a source of inspiration. Most of us probably have more nay-saying basement people in our lives than we do balcony people. That is what makes balcony people so special, and what should make us want to be balcony people for those around us. Balcony people offer hope and encouragement. Balcony people are living examples that finding meaning in life beyond ourselves is not only possible, but rewarding and invigorating. Becoming someone's balcony person is not identical with becoming intimate, but clearly, it is a step in that direction and a step in the right direction.

SUMMARY

People of hope are not free of disappointments, failures or serious challenges in their environments or relationships. Neither do they repress bad feelings and substitute those with false hope. Nor do they naively believe that everything will be okay if they do nothing but wait for things to change. But they are patient and accept limitations in the human condition, and they have a strong sense of history that allows them to see where their generation and they themselves fit into the circumstances that our ancestors left us. Their patience and understanding allow them to forgive and forgive again when things go wrong. Despite the evil and unfortunate events that occur almost daily, they still maintain a general sense of hope that something more meaningful truly is possible and that their own life is energized by pursuing intimacy with others. They understand that they can choose hope over cynicism or anger.

The person of hope looks forward to being renewed, refreshed and re-energized in a culture that tends to drown us in our own busyness.

I cannot say how everyone else can become a person of hope—there is no "one way" in a world of unique individuals. But I can say that it would not be possible for me to be a person of hope without also being a person who hopes in God, a very personal God who is not only in my balcony, but in my heart as well. God is such a special source of my hope that I must pick up this subject in the next chapter.

NOTES TO CHAPTER FOURTEEN: CHARACTERISTICS OF THE PERSON OF HOPE

1. E. R. Chamberlin, *The Bad Popes* (New York: The Dial Press, Inc., 1969), 70.

2. Will and Ariel Durant, *The Lessons of History* (New York: Simon and Schuster, 1968), 91-92 and 102.

3. Gail Sheehy, *Pathfinders* (New York: William Morrow and Company, Inc., 1981), 50-53.

4. Erik H. Erikson, *The Life Cycle Completed* (New York: W. W. Norton & Company, 1982), 56-61.

5. *Ibid.*, 79.

6. John Powers, *Mirror, Mirror on the Wall: The Art of Talking With Yourself* (Mystic, Connecticut: Twenty-Third Publications, 1987), 60.

7. See Dr. Elisabeth Kubler-Ross, *On Death and Dying* (New York: Macmillan, 1969).

A CRISIS OF HOPE

8. John Powers, *Mirror, Mirror on the Wall,* 61.

9. Martin Padovani, *Healing Wounded Emotions* (Mystic, Connecticut: Twenty-Third Publications, 1987), 38-39.

10. Henri Nouwen, *The Way of the Heart* (New York: Ballantine Books, 1981), 10.

11. *Ibid.,* 15.

12. Clayton Barbeau's public address, August 10, 1985, at the national convention of the Christian Family Movement in Notre Dame, Ind.

13. Joyce Landorf Heatherley, *Balcony People* (Austin, Texas: Balcony Publishing, 1984), 33.

14. *Ibid.,* 69.

CHAPTER FIFTEEN

Hope in God

I DID not tell the whole story in the last chapter when discussing the importance of solitude. I did not do justice to Henri Nouwen's explanation in *The Way of the Heart* of the purpose of solitude. While challenging us to face our own "nothingness" in silence in times of solitude, he goes on to say, "We enter into solitude first of all to meet our Lord and to be with him and him alone . . . only with a single-minded attention to Christ can we give up our clinging fears and face our own true nature."[1]

Adding the concept of hoping in God—the God whose son Jesus redeemed the world and is therefore my savior, too—to the other attributes of the person of hope, significantly and permanently changes my outlook on the person of hope. I imagine it is possible to be a person of hope without a belief in God, but not for me. For me, the person of hope is a person who prays, probably imperfectly, probably not all of the time, and probably in a manner that is interrupted by intermittent periods of weeks or months in which the prayer does not happen very often or very easily.

Nouwen suggests in *The Wounded Healer* that it is in the solitude of our prayer that we learn to articulate the inner feelings and the spiritual movements of our inner life. Learning to identify and articulate what is happening on the inside is what happens to the person of hope. In fact, Nouwen adds,

A CRISIS OF HOPE

"the first and most basic task of the Christian leader in the future will be to lead his people out of the land of confusion and into the land of hope. Therefore, he must first have the courage to be an explorer of the new territory in himself and to articulate his discoveries as a service to the inward generation."[2]

I have been in the land of confusion, and from time to time, I go back there. I have doubted God, doubted myself, doubted others. This should be no revelation at all for the person of hope who has a sense of history. My spiritual journey contains no dramatic moments like getting knocked off a horse. It contains no miraculous turnarounds; I am not a former drug dealer, convict, playboy, or celebrity atheist. My journey is much less dramatic than the testimony of people who can spellbind audiences with tales of miraculous healings or near-miraculous eleventh hour interventions by God. Mine is not a story of being snatched from quicksand moments before the devil would have had a permanent hold on me.

No, my upbringing, like that of many baby boomers, was large-family, white, suburban middle class. Parochial grade school and high school, a college education at a state university, followed by marriage, kids, a few jobs and a mortgage or two. It is a story over which I had little control in the early years and few regrets about now. Even my spiritual journey has a certain ho-humness about it, because there was never a time that my faith in God or participation in church waned considerably, as it does almost like clockwork in many adolescents and young adults. I am not suggesting that my faith has always been primary in my life. It hasn't; perhaps it rarely has been *primary*. But I always have lived with some sense that God is real and alive in the world. I have no regrets about that, either.

My adult understanding of God involves a gradual realization that God is much more than an important figure or participant in world history. He is much more than the figure around whom organized religions are based. He is not only a God of the intellect and organized religion, but also a God of the heart—a God who has knocked on every heart of every person in history. My adult relationship with this God has been an unclear mixture of "doing religious things" in the context of organized religion, presumably for God's sake, and living as if he *really is here,* beside me and with me, to guide me. I still struggle intermittently, not with making faith *most* important in my life, as the cliches tell us it should be, but simply with having it *among* the priorities of my life. Too often I catch myself fitting God into my schedule, just as I fit in a child's ballgame, instead of truly living every moment assured of God's presence. Just as there are stages in history and stages in adult development and stages in relationships with other people, so, too, are there stages in this relationship with God. Hope becomes an essential ingredient in appreciating and working through all of these stages of faith development.

To hope in anything less than God will always be a short-sighted hope, for only in God is there life that is most meaningful, if not most deeply satisfying. Knowing that God is here and alive and a participant in our human condition should give us a foundation not to back away from the challenges of the modern world, but to look for reasons in the modern world to have hope.

A CRISIS OF HOPE

The God who is also known as Love, as the source of our hope, ultimately becomes the reason that hope means searching beyond ourselves for something more meaningful in life. Our search leads us to God, although at times we may not recognize him. Oftentimes it begins as a more general kind of spiritual search that is hard to articulate; in fact, these inner groanings that are a part of every person's spiritual journey may float around undefined for many years. For people with an expressed belief in God, the journey never stops, and therefore there are always some unsettling spiritual feelings emanating from God and in need of clarification, through solitude and reflection. Because the God of Love is also the personal God of every person with whom I come in contact, my search for God also leads me to attempt to love others and become intimate with others in friendship. Hence, God is the source of unity among people.

Hope is a central theme of the Bible and all of Christian history. The word hope shows up more than 160 times in the Bible, where stories of God's prophets who rely on hope are abundant. Hope is often connected to times of weakness, conflict or affliction. "[W]e even boast of our afflictions," Paul bluntly told the early Christian community at Rome, "knowing that affliction produces endurance, and endurance, proven character, and proven character, hope, and hope does not disappoint, because the love of God has been poured out into our hearts through the holy Spirit that has been given to us" (Romans 5:3-5).

The great saints of history clearly had this sense of hope deeply ingrained, and they endured great challenges, strengthened more by hope in God than anything else. They also had great faith, of course, but my hunch is that they lived in hope that God would prevail even more than they had faith that any specific thing would be accomplished by their efforts. Because the circumstances in which many saints lived were antagonistic and dangerous, they undoubtedly had to live with the kind of hope whose outcome could not be known. "I consider that the sufferings of this present time are as nothing compared with the glory to be revealed to us," Paul wrote. "For in hope we are saved. Now hope that sees for itself is not hope. For who hopes for what one sees? But if we hope for what we do not see, we wait with endurance" Romans 8:18, 24-25).

Stephen, the first Christian martyr whose faith-filled death is described in the Acts of the Apostles, could not have known that his example of suffering would be repeated by other followers of Jesus for 1,950 years and still counting. He preached about his Lord with great wisdom and spirit (Acts 6:10), and as he was being stoned by those who could not accept his teachings, he asked for forgiveness of his persecutors. "Lord, do not hold this sin against them," he said (Acts 7:60). Clearly, his martyrdom was an act of hope as well as an example of courage.

For anyone who chooses to have hope in God, the hard questions never go away. It is important, in fact, that they stay: Does God cause the problems and tension in our lives? The bad luck, the poverty, the arguments with other people? Earthquakes, hurricanes and famine? Divorce, sickness and bitter family quarrels? Political turmoil, wars and racial hatred? Emotional violence, sexism in the workplace, factory closings?

A CRISIS OF HOPE

Why should we have hope in God, any god, when all of these others things that so easily stir our anger are going on? Where is God in all of this?

To answer the hard questions honestly, the first requirement is that cliches be avoided. Spinning off a phrase such as "It must be God's will" or "Everything happens for a reason" will not satisfy us, and in many cases of hardship it may not be true, anyway, as I explained in Chapter 13 in a discussion of bad luck. No, for hope to be hope it must not be superficial, but something deeply ingrained in our bones.

I do not believe God sends turmoil or disaster into my life, and neither does he *allow* them in the sense that he is deliberately sending a test or punishment for my own good. But he does allow them to the extent that these things are a part of the human condition in which we have a great deal of freedom, and part of what happens is because of Mother Nature and because of how we humans choose to relate to one another.

God—always God, always omnipotent, always the One defined as Love—has chosen to participate in our human condition. Jesus is here—the incarnational God—with a kingdom not of this world but ever in search of a loving relationship with me. He is, in fact, always more eager to love me than I am to love him. He is nearby, always ready to suggest, always ready to guide, always ready to love when I am rejoicing and when I am hurting. I still remember a critical day in high school when I told a priest that I was no longer sure if I believed in God. His calm and simple response was that doubts are quite normal. He suggested that I ask God

181

in prayer if he were really there, really here. If not, then my question would prove to be a very good one, and if he is, well, God would let me know somehow. So I did take that question to prayer. I cannot say exactly how God answered, but the stirrings in my heart, difficult to articulate later, helped me realize that God is alive in the world.

I wish the heart's spiritual stirrings were easier to transcribe, that it were possible to tell one story or provide one vivid description to prove what I know is true. But the fact is, the foundation of every person's relationship with God is going to have its own nuances, because the relationship is very personal and based on one's unique biography.

One hard-to-explain reality about a relationship with God is that life is not one long stroll through a garden of berries and fragrant roses. Jesus himself told us how challenging it would be when he said bluntly, "If anyone wishes to come after me, he must deny himself and take up his cross daily and follow me. For whoever wishes to save his life will lose it, but whoever loses his life for my sake will save it" (Luke 9:23-24). Never did he say that a friendship with him would produce a life without stress or a permanent state of immediate gratification. On the contrary, just as life includes painful circumstances, so does a relationship with God—a life in pursuit of love—include the cross.

This makes it more difficult to summarize what it means to live with hope in God. It means accepting crosses in our lives, yes, but they are crosses that build character and give us, as Paul said, a "hope that does not disappoint." I like the basic approach of the Teens Encounter Christ movement, which preaches the basic Christian tenet that our lives are spiraling with times of "death" and "resurrection," of sinning and turning away from sin. This is commonly called the "paschal mystery." Jesus lived the most profound example of what it means to experience resurrection. His powerful conquering of death laid the foundation for everything else that will happen in human history. His words that conclude Matthew's Gospel are among my favorite in the Bible: "I am with you always, until the end of the age" (Matthew 28:20). Since I take these words seriously, I believe that Jesus is here, today, now. That means, profoundly and necessarily, that everything else is affected.

These are profound statements of faith that over time, also become statements of hope. Sociologist and Baptist pastor Anthony Compolo, in his book *It's Friday, but Sunday's Comin'*, tells a terrific story about what it means to have Christian hope. He was one of seven preachers sharing the pulpit during a Good Friday service, and describes how his pastor used one line during a 90-minute sermon that turned on the congregation:[3]

That one line was "It's Friday, but Sunday's comin'!" That statement may not blow you away, but you should have heard him do it. He started his sermon real softly by saying, "It was Friday; it was Friday and my Jesus was dead on the tree. But that was Friday, and Sunday's comin'.

The preacher kept going. He picked up the volume still more and shouted, "It was Friday. The cynics were lookin' at the world and sayin', 'As things have been so they shall be. You can't change anything in this world; you can't

183

change anything.' But those cynics didn't know that it was only Friday. Sunday's comin'!

"It was Friday! And on Friday, those forces that oppress the poor and make the poor to suffer were in control. But that was Friday! Sunday's comin'!

"It was Friday, and on Friday Pilate thought he had washed his hands of a lot of trouble. The Pharisees were struttin' around and laughin' and pokin' each other in the ribs. They thought they were back in charge of things, but they didn't know that it was only Friday! Sunday's comin!''

By the time he had come to the end of the message, I was exhausted. He had made me and everybody else so worked up that I don't think any of us could have stood it much longer. At the end of his message he just yelled at the top of his lungs, "IT'S FRIDAY!'' and all five hundred of us in that church yelled back with one accord, "SUNDAY'S COMIN'!''

That is a sermon of hope. Friday to Sunday. Death to resurrection. Hurt feelings and pain and suffering to hope. The cross to new life. Sunday's comin'!

To hope in God is the ultimate statement of hope, because it is an acknowledgment that we are mortal and that only God is God. To hope in God gives our lives a new, refreshing perspective, because it allows us to interact with others and seemingly hopeless circumstances with an attitude that we must do the best we can but the results of our efforts are not ours to determine. Nor should we want them to be, because only God is God! Without such hope, it is so easy to be chained down or bitter about a lack of progress in matters important to us. To hope in God, therefore, teaches us the kind of patience that is essential for the person of hope.

NOTES TO CHAPTER FIFTEEN: HOPE IN GOD

1. Henri Nouwen, *The Way of the Heart* (New York: Ballantine Books, 1981), 17.

2. Nouwen, *The Wounded Healer* (Garden City, New York: Image Books, a division of Doubleday & Company, Inc., 1972), 38-40.

3. Anthony Compolo, *It's Friday, but Sunday's Comin'* (Waco, Texas: Word Books, 1984), 117-119.

CHAPTER SIXTEEN

Hope in the (Institutional) Church

I CAN almost see people poised anxiously on the sidelines, waiting for me to address the question: Should people who hope in God also have hope in the kind of organized religion usually identified as the institutional church? Is the church worthy of our hope? These questions are interesting precisely because most people know that institutional churches are imperfect; people who run them are imperfect; and people who experience these institutions intimately have in-depth knowledge of the imperfections. The questions are so interesting because the real question is this: Should people who hope in God also have hope in an institution that is not always worthy of their unqualified hope and support?

My answer, ultimately, is yes, but it's not a simple yes. It's not a black-and-white yes. It's gray. It's a yes that requires a careful explanation, some clear definitions, and some qualifications.

Once when I was a participant at a major assembly of the Catholic Church at the diocesan (regional) level, the guest speaker asked us to consider three questions that I had trouble answering definitively. I still do. The three questions: Is this church worth *working for,* either as a paid employee or as an active voluntary member? Is this church worth *sacrificing for?* Is this church worth *suffering for?*

A CRISIS OF HOPE

I was disappointed by the speaker's quick conclusion that our mere presence at the assembly provided positive proof of our "overwhelming yes." Maybe he was trying to flatter us, but his willingness to answer so quickly to such profound questions was just too simplistic. It's not that simple. It cannot be that simple—and the answer cannot be exactly the same for several hundred people in any church.

First of all, any discussion about "the church" requires a clear definition. Most of the time in our everyday conversation, church means the institutions of organized religion, which are usually established at both the local level and national and/or international levels. For simplicity here, I divide organized religion into seven categories: Jewish, mainline Protestant, Catholic, Muslim, Buddhist, evangelical/fundamentalist Protestant, and all others. But limiting my definition of church to organized religion is not sufficient, because there are numerous spinoffs and variations and models of these main categories. To identify just a few:

- Parachurch groups: There are numerous parachurch organizations, not connected directly to any denomination but nonetheless defined as operating on religious principles. Many prayer groups, street ministries, counseling services and social action groups often have leaders who are also active members in one of the organized religions.
- Cults: Often on the fringe of society, cults nonetheless remain a major player because of their ability to attract members and coerce them into giving up much of their valuable time and money, if not their lives.
- Religious broadcasters and publishers: To reach mass

187

audiences, a few television ministries and numerous radio stations and religious publishing houses generally seek as their customers people who belong to churches. While publishers and radio stations cover the spectrum of religious beliefs, television ministries for the most part have been dominated by Christian fundamentalist preachers. The future of these TV preachers seemed uncertain as the 1980s came to an end, with scandals involving Jim Baker and Jimmy Swaggart spurring a national skepticism. The Arbitron ratings reported a whopping 41 percent decline in viewership of the top five television preachers (Swaggart, Robert Schuller, Oral Roberts, Jerry Falwell and Pat Robertson) from 1984 to late 1988, from 7.3 million to 4.3 million households.[1]

• The local church: At the other extreme, there is the "local church," the building found on street corners in most neighborhoods of the U.S. By "church," many people refer primarily to this local place (as in, "I'm going to church") and base their current attitude about "church" on their assessment of what's happening locally, regardless of the larger organized religion with which it is affiliated. At the grassroots level people find it easy to understand Jesus' remark that "where two or three are gathered in my name, there am I in the midst of them" (Matthew 18:20).

• As Avery Dulles explained in his landmark book, *Models of the Church,* even within an institution, different members have vastly different ideas of why the institution is important. Some focus on the church as an *institution* that makes the rules; others on the church as a *servant* to the poor and needy; others on the church as a *community* of believers; still others on the church as a public *herald* of the gospel, and so on.[2] Members who have a strong inclination toward the institutional model might be moved toward administration or toward trying to get everybody else to obey the rules, while those who favor the servant model might live in a poor neighborhood and place little emphasis on pronouncements from denominational head-quarters.

The existence of so many models and variations of "church" makes it essential to identify clearly which definition of church I am using. So I return to my earlier statement that in common parlance, "the church" often refers generally to organized religion such as United Methodist or Catholic, either at the local or superstructural level. It is this definition that I am using in asking the question: Is the church worthy of our hope?

Ken Woodward, the longtime religion writer for *Newsweek,* once observed in a speech that the church looks much better to him from mid-range than from close range.[3] In other words, from a distance the church appears to do many things very well, but up close, it doesn't look so good. I will point out in the next chapter that such an insight may be true not only of the church, but of every major social structure and organization and business with which we become involved. This has terribly important implications for the person of hope. The attractiveness of the church is that it helps people contact the divine, but the church's unattractiveness lies in its human flaws.

Knowing this, I still chuckled when I heard Woodward joke about the church's internal problems in his remarks to a group of Catholic communications specialists. They knew all too well that the church's general reputation from mid-range is that of a stable, helpful organization that builds institutions, sets rules, makes pronouncements and generally tries to assist those who are down and out. From close range, however, the church's paid employees also know the church suffers from every kind of organizational ailment: poor communication, inconsistent leadership, bureaucratic delays, and gaffes never made public. I have seen church employees let go or be moved out of their positions with no regard for their dignity. I have seen the spirits of many church members, clergy and laity alike, occasionally crushed by cruel remarks or indifference from their fellow church members. I have felt stymied myself, after proposing an idea or offering my services for a particular project, by a slow response or total lack of response from people in authority.

And, lest I seem to place myself on a pedestal, I have on occasion been the reason that someone else felt wounded by the church. I especially remember one time, while the editor of a Catholic newspaper, when I responded in print to a letter to the editor by deliberately embarrassing the letter writer. It felt good for a moment, but later I felt a need to apologize publicly and then privately to the individual. Although she forgave me, I'll bet that person occasionally uses me as an example of how insensitive church leaders can be.

Lay church employees are not alone in experiencing such problems. So do many ordained ministers and others who have dedicated their lives to full-time ministry, only to find themselves left too alone by their superiors or without adequate support from their peers or their congregations.

Also feeling pains inflicted by others in church settings are many devoted regular members who become active volunteers or officers in church organizations and boards. My experience has been primarily with the Catholic Church, but I feel comfortable in saying most other churches, if not all, struggle with the same kinds of human problems. The reason is simple: All members of all churches have human weaknesses, and human weaknesses do not discriminate on account of religious preference. Even from mid-range, people grumble about the church—*their* church, any kind, anywhere. They complain about their pastor and they gossip about other church members and church leaders. They get bent out of shape by the person two rows behind them who wouldn't stop talking during the service. And they mumble everywhere that things could be better if only people would get along better and the people and ministers would work together better. Generally that attitude can be translated as, ''Things would be better if more people rallied around my point of view.''

The church's flaws are so obvious—so obvious that I am tempted to go on indefinitely, trying to prove beyond a reasonable doubt that I know what I'm talking about. But move on I must. As I move into a discussion about hope in the church, I will neither dismiss nor lose sight of the church's flaws. I am frequently in contact with people who feel wounded by the church, or who see it as behind the times or irrelevant rather than on the prophetic edge of change in the world. I know that the instant I move into a discussion about hope in the church, some will want to interrupt me and say, "Yes, but . . ." And I will be glad to listen, over and over again, but still, personally, I must move on.

The alternative to having hope is living in a perpetual state of anger, frustration, despair, bitterness or cynicism. The alternative to having hope in the church is not having hope in the church, which means going it alone, dropping out, or changing churches or forming new churches if you don't like the one you're in. I have known people who responded in one or more of these ways, and I refuse to be a quick judge of their choices. Usually they make them with much anguish, their reasoning is complex, and the decision may not be permanent anyway.

To declare that hope in the institutional church is a better alternative is not the same as saying persons should swallow everything the church feeds them, flaws and all, or that challenges to the status quo are always inappropriate. To say "I don't have hope in the church but I'll hang in there and see if I can make a difference" is actually a statement of hope.

Getting back to basics, I cannot discuss hope in the church without first recalling the general characteristics of the person of hope: a sense of history, patience, humility, an inclination to forgive, hope in oneself, and hope in others. Add to that hoping in God, which is where one's hope ultimately rests, and then keep in mind that the Christian church is one that teaches the divine God (Jesus) became one of us, and still lives among us and within our hearts.

The person of hope looks at the church with a sense of history and a forgiving heart. History teaches that the church was entrusted with spreading the Good News first proclaimed by Jesus from one generation to the next, from the Apostles on down, century after century. In the process of doing that, the church has had inspiring moments of glory as well as significant embarrassments. In its most inspiring times, the church helps people see meaning that is beyond themselves. It helps people move in the direction of intimacy with God above all else, for he is the source of their hope. He is the source of hope.

On a more concrete level, here are just three ways in which the institutional church has made and continues to make positive contributions to individuals and to the world:

- It has nourished the lives of individual believers throughout history. Through its designated leaders such as ordained and anointed ministers, it has been present to people at many of their most significant moments, such as births, weddings and funerals. It has been present to comfort them, feed them and educate them in the name of the Lord, and of course, always within the limitations of the knowledge and culture of the era.

- It has existed on the prophetic edge of change while immersing itself in contemporary culture. The church now has a unique position from which to speak out in defense of human rights in Central America and South Africa, and against the horrifying consequences of the buildup of nuclear arms. At the local level, churches take leadership roles in feeding hungry people, offering hospitality to the homeless, and erecting a kind of imaginary gigantic viewing area with special glass so that all of us can see contemporary society in the light of biblical principles. "For I was hungry and you gave me food, I was thirsty and you gave me drink, a stranger and you welcomed me, naked and you clothed me, ill and you cared for me, in prison and you visited me . . . Amen I say to you, whatever you did for one of these least brothers of mine, you did for me'' (Matthew 25:35-36, 40). The church's challenge is clear, and it has responded.

• It has also provided a cultural and spiritual foundation for people's lives by being the place not only for worship, but also for many local social functions in church buildings and halls on the street corners of most neighborhoods. The church so often is taken for granted as a central point around which its members' personal activities and lifestyle are built.

For one to have a sense of the church's historical developments offers a foundation for hope, although I must be careful to say the hope lies not in the accomplishments themselves but in the church's unique role in bridging the gap between the human and the divine.

An absence of a sense of the church's continuous movement through history, on the other hand, can be a cause of temporary or permanent disillusionment. Catholics on the far right, for example, are relentless in trying to convince everybody else that the church is going down the drain because too many others are not as dismayed as they are about the rapid changes in the church since the Second Vatican Council ended in 1965. Sometimes such pleadings are accompanied by suggestions to revert to pre-Vatican II practices such as the Tridentine (traditional Latin) Mass. Because the far right finds hope mostly in the past, it faces the risk of disillusionment.

People on the left take a similar risk, but for them utter frustration sets in when the church does not make changes quickly enough, which for them, is most of the time. Since *they* don't mind being on the edge of change, they want *everybody else* to join them in their prophetic stances, right or wrong. They get discouraged when this does not happen immediately, and if they fail to recognize that living on the edge means by definition going it alone for awhile, they quickly blame the world's institutions for falling behind, and therefore also face the risk of disillusionment.

Most people are between these two extremes. The person with a holy hope condemns neither those on the right nor those on the left but learns from each side. From the right one learns the importance of remaining rooted in traditions ("a sense of history"), and from the left one is reminded that change is always necessary and improvement is often possible. The person of hope understands that human nature is always going to place a small percentage of people on both the far left and far right. The person of hope has the humility to understand that you can never be too sure that you are right, and that even when you are, you usually can't be absolutely certain that you are. Henri Nouwen explains, in *With Open Hands,* the great sensitivity of the person of hope:

> He is happy and glad to have people listen to him, but he is not out to form groups around himself, to build an organization or to launch a movement. No cliques can grow up around him, for he attaches himself exclusively to no

195

one. What he says and does has a convincing ring and even a self-evident truth, but he forces his opinions on no one and is not annoyed when someone doesn't adopt his opinion or doesn't do as he wishes.

In everything, he seems to have a concrete and living goal in mind, the realization of which is of vital importance. Yet he himself maintains a great inner freedom in the light of this goal. Often it seems as though he knows that he will never see the goal achieved, and that he only sees the shadow of it himself. But, throughout, he has an impressive freedom from the course of his own life. He is careful and cautious, certainly not reckless, and yet it comes out at every turn that he counts his life as of secondary importance.[4]

So the person with hope in the institutional church is not a mindless follower. Not naive. Not foolish. And not without risks, even the risks of disillusionment and rejection.

The humility connected with this kind of hope cannot be overemphasized. One aspect of humility, as Nouwen suggested, is not to take ourselves too seriously, and one way of doing that is by rediscovering a sense of humor in the church. "A sense of humor, like a sense of humility, involves ruthless honesty about who we are without disguise or pretense," theologian Doris Donnelly said. "The temptation, of course, is to become weighted with gravity; the grace is to face ourselves with an appropriate degree of levity."[5] The same day she made these remarks in a lecture, she also explained that humor can be a great, healthy tool for lightening the load of pain and suffering:

A CRISIS OF HOPE

Take inventory of a situation causing pain. How could it be approached or resolved differently if a sense of humor were operative? . . . Humor doesn't deny the hurt; it is the vehicle through which anger and defiance and pain are handled.

When a friend of mine, the mother of four young sons, was dying of cancer, she told her children, "When I die, you should be able to count on God for at least a hundred special favors." After she died, the boys found the following note addressed to each individually. "I changed my mind. You each have a thousand special favors. (Signed) God."[6]

As I think about the conflicts and arguments that take place in the institutional church, I amuse myself with how many serious differences of opinion could be defused if somebody, on either side, would only add a bit of humor to the discussion—laughing at oneself instead of the rival party. I find this especially effective in ecumenical circles, when I can laugh about the seriousness with which my Catholic Church takes some of its customs that my Protestant sisters and brothers find rather meaningless.

To be a person of hope means having hope in ourselves, in others and in God. Since the community of believers with God in their midst is a good definition of "church," it therefore becomes possible to say that it's appropriate to have hope in the institutional church. Having hope means having hope despite all of the obstacles that stand in the way of a perfect world. Having hope means having hope despite all of the specific incidents and trends that make us wonder whether hope makes any sense at all.

Finally, it must be said that having hope does not mean having a high degree of hope all of the time. It means at times allowing ourselves and others real space for anger, despair and frustration—helped along, perhaps, by the assurance from God that something more meaningful in our lives is possible, but knowing that we must spend some time dealing with painful feelings. Feeling wounded in the church or by the church is not unusual or inappropriate for the person of hope. "Dropping out" as a temporary solution might even be necessary at times, utilizing the withdrawal as a "sorting out time" rather than a permanent angry solution that isn't really a solution.

It may be intellectually misleading to ask that persons of hope find a conclusive *rational* basis for having hope in the institutional church, because the prerequisites would be a faith and hope in God or other higher power. Such a hope, of course, requires a process that ultimately goes beyond reason; it is the kind of commitment that I find quite reasonable and real but that many others reject for a variety of reasons.

The absence of a rationale, however, does not preclude the possibility of finding good *reasons* for finding hope in organized religion. Some of them I mentioned earlier—the ways in which the church has inspired and nourished people over the years, and the church's ability to provide an anchor of stability even on the edge of change. From this perspective the church is calling on us to look within ourselves and beyond ourselves for what is more meaningful in life, and to help us grow and develop as individuals. The church is calling on us as individuals to have hope in something beyond ourselves—namely, God. From this vantage point the church is effective at calling us to be inspired by God to be the salt of the earth.

That is why it makes sense to have hope in the institution whose unique responsibility it is to be a witness of hope. The hope really is in God, within the structure of the institutionalized church. Persons of hope are aware of the church's positive influence on people and society, and hope in the church becomes natural for the person who has learned to appreciate the value of history and learned not to demand perfection.

The person of hope is neither satisfied nor dissatisfied with the way things are. The person of hope is neither satisfied nor dissatisfied with the way the church is, but has hope in its message and witness of hope.

NOTES TO CHAPTER SIXTEEN:
HOPE IN THE (INSTITUTIONAL) CHURCH

1. Randy Frame, "Religious Broadcasting: Will It Survive the Slump?" *Christianity Today,* 3 Feb. 1989, cover graph and pages 32-34.

2. Avery Dulles, S. J., *Models of the Church* (New York: Doubleday, 1974).

3. Ken Woodward, the senior religion writer for *Newsweek* magazine, made these remarks at the national convention of

Ed Wojcicki

Unda-USA, the organization of Catholic communications specialists, in November 1987 in Tampa, Florida.

4. Henri Nouwen, *With Open Hands* (Notre Dame, Indiana: Ave Maria Press, 1972), 134.

5. Doris Donnelly, "The Blessing Called Humor," *Origins* (Washington, D.C.: NC Documentary Service), 5 May 1988, 810.

6. *Ibid.*, 812.

CHAPTER SEVENTEEN

Hope in the Marketplace and the Government

A DISCUSSION about hope would not be honest unless it takes into account some areas of life with which we are quite familiar: the economy in which people work and buy things, and the government in which we are all participants and from which we all receive services. If I cannot have hope while in the routine of my work and my life, then my whole notion of hope is of little value.

Just as I began the last chapter by talking about the church's flaws, so do I find it easy here to note the obvious. Attitudes in the general American public about businessmen and politicians and corporations often are unfavorable, if not hostile. The word "businessman" can quickly raise an image of an insensitive character interested only in profits, and "politician" the thought of someone who cannot be trusted and whose only real interest is winning elections. How easy it is to find real-life examples to support these stereotypes. How easy it is to become suspicious, angry and cynical. How reasonable it is to be outraged by scandals and immoral conditions, such as:

—All-too-frequent incidents of sexual harrassment and racial and sexual discrimination in an era when these things are no longer supposed to happen. One of the saddest stories I ever had to follow as a reporter was that of a rural township supervisor who eventually went to prison for using

201

township welfare funds as leverage to get poor women to do sexual favors for him. Things like that aren't supposed to happen on the laid-back main streets of small towns, but unfortunately, they do.

—The switch by tobacco companies in their marketing to lure more women and minority customers, due to the declining number of white male smokers—despite the overwhelming evidence that smoking causes cancer.[1]

—Frequent overbuying and overspending by governments either to satisfy political friends or to make sure the whole budget gets spent before the fiscal year ends.

—Loyal workers advancing in age getting laid off or fired because it's cheaper for the company to hire young employees for less money.

—Ample evidence of hunger and starvation in Africa.

—The cycles of poverty that keep millions of people in the Third World and in America's inner cities living in less-than-humane conditions. Neither political nor economic solutions have yet been found. Nor are they likely to be found in my lifetime.

—The relatively frequent exposés of political scandals, such as those of presidential candidate Gary Hart in 1987-88, and the Iran-Contra scandal during that same time period.

—The all-too-frequent stories of government violence against innocent citizens, stories coming out of China, Sri Lanka, Cambodia, and South Africa, for example.

The longer such a list gets, the more appropriate it becomes for the reasonable person to say that only a fool could have

A CRISIS OF HOPE

hope in the world's malfunctioning economic and political structures. I will not attempt to prove otherwise. I will not attempt to prove there ought to be hope in the world of business or in the government. I will not attempt to show that the systems themselves are largely moral, compassionate or operating smoothly, because they are not. But they are not inherently immoral, either. As persons of hope operate within these structures, as they must do, they can maintain a high degree of hope that something better is possible and that something more meaningful is available to them. My focus is on these persons of hope.

For the person of hope in every arena, the starting point is a sense of history. Robert Spencer, a former Vermont state senator who became a political science professor and university president, once created an upper-level course on political cynicism at Sangamon State University in Springfield, Illinois. He used literary, philosophical and other texts to explore why people almost universally mistrust political and social institutions. Citing a prevailing cynicism in the modern world, he laments that too few citizens believe they have an obligation to public service, when the very premise of the American form of government is that we are capable of governing ourselves.

Spencer's premise is itself a statement of optimism and hope—that we can govern ourselves, and everybody has some role in the process. The point of his course on political cynicism was to help his students find legal, ethical and environmental ingredients with which to create workable, believable political communities. The fact that he would call his course "Political Cynicism, Hypocrisy and Alienation" is signal enough that he is aware of the bad rap that politicians usually get. But he confidently adds that being a citizen requires some form of public service. One cannot be both a good citizen and a cynic, he says, because cynicism becomes a copout that stops people from trying to make a difference. So much does he believe in this that he considers himself a failure if his students do not enter public life within ten years after taking his courses. Among those for whom he takes some credit is U.S. Senator Pat Leahy, the Vermont Democrat.[2]

Spencer is especially concerned about the portrayal of people by television news, which often does not distinguish between human weakness and evil corruption. Television generally uses some form of human weakness as the basis of its stories—weaknesses such as bad judgment, conflicts between people, and immorality. Spencer says that to have so many stories founded on human weakness, day after day and year after year, gradually paints a picture of the human race and its institutions as woefully lacking and falling impossibly short of the idealized world that television itself has created. That's why Spencer's perspective is so important:

> Unless you see it as human weakness instead of utter corruption, you're going to be a cynic. If you see things as human weakness you have a capacity to forgive. But if you see it as a corrupt government, you've signed off. We're not obliged to become cynics; we're obliged to become citizens. Being a good citizen takes time away from baseball, trivia, computer games, beer—the time required to be a serious listener to public discourse. There are many

A CRISIS OF HOPE

barriers to committing ourselves to public life, and one of the neatest barriers that excuses us is cynicism.[3]

Public service, either as an elected official or as a political activist at any level, involves sacrifices in one's private life. The person of hope may not feel obliged to be the one who runs for office, but neither is the person of hope so cynical about government that he or she believes it no longer deserves our participation or our interest. The person of hope sees the government as a structure within which positive things for the common good can be accomplished, although rarely as quickly or as neatly as we would like. People of hope have to persevere to get anywhere in politics, especially with the big causes. For more than 100 years in the U.S., for example, women did not have the right to vote—they got this fundamental right only in 1920 with the ratification of the Nineteenth Amendment. Fifty years earlier, in 1870, blacks received the right to vote after finally receiving legal status as people just a few years earlier. In one sense these historical reminders are like embarrassing black eyes in our history; in another sense they are reminders that people of hope are not out of line in yearning for something better, even when the moral and political winds are gusting in their faces with hurricane force.

It is the optimist's task to live as if something better really is possible.

It is the task of the person of hope, who may or may not be an optimist, to find meaning for a different reason.

For persons of hope, the meaning comes not from a mission accomplished, not from progress, and not from a hint

205

of success. No, the meaning emanates from *their own personal response* to those inner, often unclear urgings that remind them that something better is possible and that something more meaningful in life is possible. The meaning comes from accepting these urgings as real, and not fleeing from them. The meaning comes from translating these feelings into attitudes and activity that allow further exploration of what it is in life that is beyond themselves and greater than themselves.

Am I, then, subtly advocating *not working for change* or not getting involved in politics or the government? Not at all! In fact, persons equipped with hope have an invaluable tool to help them persevere and hang in there for the long haul. They know that pursuing political solutions to great social problems such as hunger, crime and discrimination of many kinds is automatically going to include many detours and many frustrations because there is no definitive, perfect solution. Their hope allows them to take on the task anyway, because their general search for meaning leads them in the direction of other people, and moves them to try to be of assistance to people in need. Their hope moves them to love.

Two cliches come quickly to mind in my reflections on hope in the government and hope in the marketplace. The cliches are admittedly contradictory, and they apply to both the government and the economy. The first is "You can't fight city hall." There are many corollaries of this. The bureaucrats don't care; they are incompetent. The repairman doesn't really care about fixing the leak in my roof; all he wants to do is make a profit by working at my house. Politicians only care about getting re-elected. Most bosses don't really care about their employees. The government doesn't really care about the people. You might as well put up with lousy service because nobody gives good service any more. You can't find good help any more.

The second cliche is "One person can make a difference." You can fight city hall. You can be a bureaucrat who cares. You can be a boss who cares about fairness in the marketplace and respect for one's employees. You can, as did Martin Luther King Jr., affect the conscience of an entire nation. You can be a statesman as well as a politician. You can be an honest employee who shows respect for the company and for the customers.

This is the kind of attitude that Spencer advocates by saying people ought to be good citizens, not cynics.

Remember Kitty Scanlan, the occupational therapist I quoted in the chapter on frustration? For a long time she could not convince herself that her work was as important as the doctors'. After dropping the profession for awhile, she returned to the hospital one day, and her own different attitude made a big difference. "It wasn't the people higher up who didn't recognize the importance of our work," she said. "It was *I* who didn't recognize it . . . Through working on this job I'm coming to learn that I do have some influence, at least over my own happiness."[4]

I admire people who try to make a difference in whatever ways they can. Mother Teresa of Calcutta has battled overwhelming problems of sickness and starvation in India by loving just one needy person at a time. Habitat for Humanity, an organization that uses volunteer labor to build houses for homeless people, isn't solving the monumental problem of thousands of people living on the streets, but it is giving homeless families a decent place to live, one house at a time.

Most people are not called to take on the great global problems as much as they are to make a difference in their own communities. I know of one couple who own a store and have such a commitment to the community that they voluntarily donate 10 percent of every sale to a local charity of the customer's preference. Another man I know, in the insurance business, gives his customers bookmark-sized ribbons with a list of potential worries in life—and biblical references to soothe the concerns. Distributing the ribbons is a quiet kind of ministry for him; he subtly asks his customers to have a broader perspective on life. "When you worry," the ribbon advises, check out Matthew 6:19-34. I did look it up one day and was reminded that flowers do no work, yet they have more splendor than King Solomon in all of his robes. "If God so clothes the grass of the field, which grows today and is thrown into the oven tomorrow," Jesus said, "will he not much more provide for you, O you of little faith? . . . Do not worry about tomorrow; tomorrow will take care of itself" (Matthew 6:30, 34).

One time when I had to fill a vacancy on my staff, I talked with a bright young woman who was told by her previous boss that she would never be allowed to do more than the most mundane of tasks, such as writing obituaries and brief news stories about local civic clubs. I thought otherwise, and asked if she would like to become my assistant. I loved her reaction. She only wanted to know: "Which move will work out best for me in the long run?" No question about it. She became my assistant, began writing her own column for

208

which she won a number of awards, and eventually earned another job at a metropolitan newspaper. She sensed at a critical point in her life that something more meaningful was possible if only she would give it a try. I did nothing other than give her a chance and the freedom to use her talents, and she took it from there.

I suspect this is what Tom Peters and Robert H. Waterman, Jr. were talking about in *In Search of Excellence*. They found that in America's best-run corporations, an important element was always *respect for the individual:* "These companies give people control over their destinies; they make meaning for people. They turn the average Joe and the average Jane into winners. They let, even insist that, people stick out. They accentuate the positive."[5]

To respect the individual is to respect the fact that one person can make a difference. This is what it means to have hope in the government and hope in the marketplace: not hope in the structures themselves, but hope in the individuals who live and work within such flawed structures. For the person who gives up totally on the structures, the only alternative is to wallow in bitterness or despair.

It is important to emphasize that although we can sometimes measure the progress of our personal development with successful projects or career advancements, our hope must never be measured by progress or successes. Hope requires us, simply but profoundly, to have an approach to life that says something more meaningful is always possible. The search for meaning goes on simultaneously within ourselves and beyond ourselves.

Did Lech Walesa, long before being elected president in

1990, really believe that political freedom would be a reality in Poland in his lifetime? Probably not. But he knew from the stirrings in his heart that freedom was a virtue worth pursuing. Therefore it became meaningful to pursue it against the potentially insurmountable opposition of a powerful Communist regime. One person, Walesa, a union man, went after freedom, and as a result millions of people throughout the world also felt within themselves a renewed kindling for freedom.

Our hearts instruct us that even when we fail to meet a goal, there is something deeply satisfying about trying. Hope emboldens us to try, and hope encourages us to keep trying.

Hope never stops teaching us that something beyond ourselves is more meaningful. Hope instructs us to love, and love, in turn, leads us to make sacrifices for others and for good causes.

NOTES TO CHAPTER SEVENTEEN:
HOPE IN THE MARKETPLACE AND GOVERNMENT

1. Ellen Schultz, "America's Most Admired Corporations," *Fortune,* 18 January 1988, 34.

2. Professor Robert Spencer, who lives in Petersburg, Illinois, made these remarks in a personal interview in my office May 30, 1989. Spencer is the founding president of Sangamon State University, a public affairs university, in Springfield, Illinois.

3. *Ibid.*

4. Studs Terkel, *Working* (New York: Pantheon Books, 1974), 496-497.

5. Thomas J. Peters and Robert H. Waterman, Jr. *In Search of Excellence* (New York: Harper & Row, 1982), 239.

CONCLUSION

Images of Hopelessness and Hope

ANY argument in support of hope almost immediately will elicit a flurry of objections. All too commonly we encounter persons and organizations saturated with despair, anger and bitterness. Why have hope? they cry. It's fine in theory, they say, but, but, but . . . and the objections to hope flow freely.

Indeed, no person is immune from the possibility of disillusionment. Without too much trouble, it is possible to create a composite image of the world dominated by people without hope:

—Unhappy workers who feel trapped in their jobs.

—Bosses who made it to the top but still feel unappreciated, unsatisfied, and lonely.

—Parents who worry incessantly about trying to be perfect parents, and often fear that they are failing.

—Wives and husbands who lament, "My spouse is never going to change," and who subsequently respond, "So neither will I, because the other really needs to change; I don't."

—Adults and children scarred for years by divorce.

—Voters who no longer trust anyone who holds an elected office.

—Suburbanites full of distress despite good jobs, healthy

children and more possessions than they ever dreamed of having.

—Ministers who feel like failures when they discover they cannot lead their congregations to be a perfectly happy community.

—People who say, "My minister is insensitive and therefore I refuse to go to church any more."

—Angry shoppers with sullen faces and little joy, but many packages, in huge urban malls during the Christmas season.

—Poor and homeless persons roaming the streets of America.

—Social workers run ragged by a society that won't listen to their cries for more assistance for the poor and the homeless.

—Gossiping men, gossiping women, nitpickers all.

—Athletes humiliated by an over-aggressive coach, sometimes at very young ages.

—Generous coaches who give so willingly of their time and feel so unappreciated by parents and athletes who actually are not grateful enough.

The composite picture of these images is that of people limping along, confused about life, slopping unhappily in a pool of despair. It is a world of angry, frustrated, cynical people.

In the subdued, foggy light of such a cold, shivering picture, I need to be very clear about three things *I am not saying* in making a case for hope in the modern world. First, I choose not to be an apologist for business, government, or organized religion. Second, I am not suggesting that hope in these structures or in God is the only missing ingredient in the remedy to the numerous complex social, political, and personal problems that I discuss. Third, asserting that hope is one of the antidotes to cynicism, anger and despair is not an attempt to establish hope as *the* answer on how to live a wholesome, happy life. Books are now proliferating to help people deal with their feelings, relationships, intimacy, stress and prayer. All are helpful topics and related to hope, but my focus is on hope.

Hope is essential because only hope can explain how satisfaction and fulfillment in life are possible despite the many obstacles that tempt us to give in to despair.

The first step to becoming a person of hope is *to accept* that in response to our circumstances in daily life, all of us have feelings that are uncomfortable, negative and unpleasant—and normal. Very normal. So normal that we should expect them, even welcome them! The next step is to learn to *identify* and *name* these feelings for what they are—anger, bitterness, depression, fear, disappointment, disillusionment, confusion, and so on. Still another step in the process is to *articulate* these feelings, sometimes in the privacy of our own reflection and sometimes to others. This helps us become less afraid of our feelings, even of the most negative feelings that lead us in the direction of despair. I find it very interesting that Henri Nouwen, the spiritual writer for whom hope is a major theme, says that hope is impossible unless a person has also known despair, and that despair is possible only for the person who knows what it is to hope.[1]

But articulating our feelings honestly is not enough to make us persons of hope. In understanding our own feelings, we find that those most common to us are also very intense in others. We become more accurately and more acutely aware of the feelings raging in others, and we are therefore confronted in new ways by the many, many human problems in the marketplace, in government, and in the church. Identifying such problems can spin us on a roller coaster that hurls us once again toward despair and frustration. For example, it was only after I had personally experienced and dealt with some difficult situations in my jobs that I became aware that many other people also feel so angry and frustrated in theirs. Then I had to deal with new information: It is common for people to be so frustrated. What can I do now? I ask.

Thus enters hope, a virtue badly needed as we peer into the 21st century and the next millenium. Hope is not based on an expectation that things will get better. Hope is not optimism, not positive thinking, not saying "I think I can, I think I can," over and over again, although it does not exclude these things.

In the beginning, one's hope might be closely linked to one's wishes and desires—for more material things, or improvement in performance, or an end to conflicts in the family, or a better job. Such desires are focused on "something better" and may even include some specific goals. But goal setting is not the same as hope, because with hope there is knowledge that something better, as in materially better, will never be ultimately satisfying. Obtaining more things or improving as a result of hard work can deliver satisfaction, indeed, but this feeling will always be relatively short-lived. It has been said rather frequently that most people believe they would finally have an adequate income if only they could receive a 25 percent increase—and this perception is true whether a person makes $15,000 or $55,000 a year! It is never enough.

The person of hope is neither satisfied nor dissatisfied. The person of hope understands that something better is possible, and that situations can improve as the result of individual efforts. But hope is not based on obtaining something better. Hope is accepting the present for what it is, and, more importantly, yearning for something different in the future—for something more fulfilling, more deeply satisfying.

Teachers and coaches with hope, for example, generously provide individual attention to their students, all the while knowing that the real fruits of their labors may not be known to them for decades, if ever. Employees with hope understand humbly how their efforts are closely linked to the work of others in a complex marketplace, and they balance the personal satisfaction (or lack of satisfaction) from a job with other values such as feeding a family, paying bills and being a citizen of the community. Social activists on the leading edge of nuclear disarmament or anti-abortion protests cannot know exactly where their cause is headed, but still they make themselves vulnerable on the edge of change. Churchgoers with hope appreciate the importance of being in a worshiping community even though their minister and congregation are far from the gate of perfection.

Hope is knowing that something more fulfilling is available to us, and hence to others, and hence, to the world. For hope to be real hope, it always propels us to yearn for something fulfilling that is beyond ourselves. How illuminating it is to understand that hope is not only directed at the future; it is also directed squarely at other people, particularly to make *their* lives more fulfilling or "better" or somehow more pleasant. Hope moves us to love.

Martin Luther King liked to say that if a person is a streetsweeper, "he should sweep streets even as Michelangelo painted, or Beethoven composed music, or Shakespeare wrote poetry. He should sweep streets so well that all the host of heaven and earth will pause to say 'here lived a great streetsweeper who did his job well.' "[2]

Whether one is a streetsweeper or owner of the company making streetsweeping machines or mayor of the city that owns the streets, the same image of hope is possible. Persons of hope in a variety of settings—sitting in an office, sweating in a coal mine, relaxing on the front porch, participating in a church committee meeting, spending extra minutes with a patient, carrying a picket sign, folding laundry, making a last-minute decision in the voting booth, suffering alone in pain over the breakup of the family—might find themselves with self-images that are remarkably similar.

Their hope is not dependent on their own effort, on themselves, or their successes. They know the world around them is imperfect; they themselves are imperfect contributors to their cause, employer, and family. They probably understand secretly, even with a touch of humble amusement, that their dreams will never be realized.

They also learn that the world's faults, failures and favoritism often inflict pain that causes them to react with many different kinds of feelings, including, at times, despair, frustration and confusion. First and foremost they make allies

217

Ed Wojcicki

of these feelings; then they learn to work with them rather than ignore them as they continue in their daily routines. No matter what their role is and what their contribution is, they understand that something more deeply satisfying than the effort at hand is possible.

What is more satisfying is something beyond themselves. Persons of hope get in touch with this yearning within themselves, then spend the remainder of their lives searching for the object of their yearning. One's understanding of this perceived "object of hope" may change over time, from "something better" to something less tangible such as intimacy with others, to something even more fulfilling such as a relationship with a personal God. Such a grasp of hope—craving for something more deeply satisfying—sometimes leads to heroic attitudes and behavior, as in the stories of Mahatma Gandhi in India, Lech Walesa in Poland and Martin Luther King in the United States. All three responded to a deeply felt hope by engaging in valiant struggles for freedom in political situations that were terribly oppressive.

Many throughout history—and I count myself in this group—find comfort in understanding that God is the source of this hope. God, the one who is beyond ourselves. God, known to some as a higher power that they cannot explain. God, the unseen destination of our prayer. God, for me, the one who sent his son, Jesus, to be one of us, to be with us forever, and to teach us the subtle difference between despair and hope. The Bible is in large part a story of hope, the story of God's promise of something more fulfilling for people who trust in him. Isaiah said it well:

A CRISIS OF HOPE

Do you not know or have you not heard? The Lord is the eternal God, creator of the ends of the earth. He does not faint or grow weary, and his knowledge is beyond scrutiny. He gives strength to the fainting; for the weak he makes vigor abound.

Though young men faint and grow weary, and youths stagger and fall, they that hope in the Lord will renew their strength, they will soar as with eagles' wings; they will run and not grow weary, walk and not grow faint (Isaiah 40:28-31).

God invites all people to be strengthened by having hope' in him, and therefore, by having hope, period, because he has promised to be with us no matter what. He has claimed the future for himself. That is our hope. That is why the Christian person of hope focuses not on ''something better'' but on something more deeply satisfying. Not enough people believe—and not enough Christians understand—that God is ever more willing to enter into a relationship of love with us than his people are to respond to that love. Christians ought to have hope primarily because God loves us, and because God loved us first. ''We don't have to solve our own loneliness if we are rooted in God's love,'' Nouwen says. ''We don't just love one another because we desperately need each other. Rather, we can be together in faithfulness because we are both rooted in that first love.''[3]

While hope is not an exclusively Christian virtue, it is clearly an important virtue of Christians. Hope secured by God's eternal promise of love makes it possible for me to leave you an image of the person of hope that is radically different from the composite image of worldly despair that I described earlier.

Persons of hope live in humble appreciation of themselves, of those around them, and of their life circumstances. Appreciative but never quite satisfied, they find it essential to pause every now and then to remind themselves specifically that they are indeed persons of hope. Or at least, they are moving in that direction, or at the very least, it's time to move in that direction once again. They never quite forget the pain that accompanies the obstacles to hope in their lives, and they appreciate that living as a person of hope means living with a few scars.

NOTES TO THE CONCLUSION

1. Henri Nouwen, *With Open Hands* (Notre Dame, Indiana: Ave Maria Press, 1972), 81 (where he says, "Despair is only possible for someone who knows what it means to hope.") Also "The Journey to Despair," *Praying* magazine No. 17 (where he says, "We will never know what hope is until we have tasted real despair.").

2. Martin Luther King Jr., as quoted in *The Book of Quotes* (New York: E. P. Dutton, 1979), 264.

3. Nouwen, *Praying* No. 17, 5.

ABOUT THE AUTHOR

Ed Wojcicki is a veteran journalist and a graduate of the School of Journalism at the University of Missouri-Columbia. Now living in Springfield, Illinois, he has had dozens of articles published in magazines and newspapers. He and his wife Sally, who is co-owner of an advertising and promotional display business, have two children, Sara and Luke.